Connected Mathe

D0536451

# How Likely Is It?

*Probability*

## Teacher's Guide

Glenda Lappan
James T. Fey
William M. Fitzgerald
Susan N. Friel
Elizabeth Difanis Phillips

Glenview, Illinois
Needham, Massachusetts
Upper Saddle River, New Jersey

Connected Mathematics™ was developed at Michigan State University with financial support from the Michigan State University Office of the Provost, Computing and Technology, and the College of Natural Science.

This material is based upon work supported by the National Science Foundation under Grant No. MDR 9150217.

This project was supported, in part,
by the
**National Science Foundation**
Opinions expressed are those of the authors
and not necessarily those of the Foundation

The Michigan State University authors and administration have agreed that all MSU royalties arising from this publication will be devoted to purposes supported by the Department of Mathematics and the MSU Mathematics Education Enrichment Fund.

*Photo Acknowledgements:* 11 © Harold M. Lambert/Superstock, Inc.; 17 © John Moore/The Image Works; 27 © Hazel Hankin/Stock, Boston; 39 © Michael Dwyer/Stock, Boston; 53 © Ed Fowler/UPI/Bettmann Newsphotos; 55 © Michael Tamborrino/FPG International; 57 © Dennis E. Cox/Tony Stone Images, Inc.; 58 © Michael Weisbrot/Stock, Boston

Monopoly is a trademark of Parker Brothers.

ISBN 0-13-053097-2
4 5 6 7 8 9 10   05 04 03 02

**Patricia Wagner**
Holmes Middle School

**Greg Williams**
Gundry Elementary School

*Lansing*
**Susan Bissonette**
Waverly Middle School

**Kathy Booth**
Waverly East Intermediate School

**Carole Campbell**
Waverly East Intermediate School

**Gary Gillespie**
Waverly East Intermediate School

**Denise Kehren**
Waverly Middle School

**Virginia Larson**
Waverly East Intermediate School

**Kelly Martin**
Waverly Middle School

**Laurie Metevier**
Waverly East Intermediate School

**Craig Paksi**
Waverly East Intermediate School

**Tony Pecoraro**
Waverly Middle School

**Helene Rewa**
Waverly East Intermediate School

**Arnold Stiefel**
Waverly Middle School

*Portland*
**Bill Carlton**
Portland Middle School

**Kathy Dole**
Portland Middle School

**Debby Flate**
Portland Middle School

**Yvonne Grant**
Portland Middle School

**Terry Keusch**
Portland Middle School

**John Manzini**
Portland Middle School

**Mary Parker**
Portland Middle School

**Scott Sandborn**
Portland Middle School

*Shepherd*
**Steve Brant**
Shepherd Middle School

**Marty Brock**
Shepherd Middle School

**Cathy Church**
Shepherd Middle School

**Ginny Crandall**
Shepherd Middle School

**Craig Ericksen**
Shepherd Middle School

**Natalie Hackney**
Shepherd Middle School

**Bill Hamilton**
Shepherd Middle School

**Julie Salisbury**
Shepherd Middle School

*Sturgis*
**Sandra Allen**
Eastwood Elementary School

**Margaret Baker**
Eastwood Elementary School

**Steven Baker**
Eastwood Elementary School

**Keith Barnes**
Sturgis Middle School

**Wilodean Beckwith**
Eastwood Elementary School

**Darcy Bird**
Eastwood Elementary School

**Bill Dickey**
Sturgis Middle School

**Ellen Eisele**
Sturgis Middle School

**James Hoelscher**
Sturgis Middle School

**Richard Nolan**
Sturgis Middle School

**J. Hunter Raiford**
Sturgis Middle School

**Cindy Sprowl**
Eastwood Elementary School

**Leslie Stewart**
Eastwood Elementary School

**Connie Sutton**
Eastwood Elementary School

*Traverse City*
**Maureen Bauer**
Interlochen Elementary School

**Ivanka Berskshire**
East Junior High School

**Sarah Boehm**
Courtade Elementary School

**Marilyn Conklin**
Interlochen Elementary School

**Nancy Crandall**
Blair Elementary School

**Fran Cullen**
Courtade Elementary School

**Eric Dreier**
Old Mission Elementary School

**Lisa Dzierwa**
Cherry Knoll Elementary School

**Ray Fouch**
West Junior High School

**Ed Hargis**
Willow Hill Elementary School

**Richard Henry**
West Junior High School

**Dessie Hughes**
Cherry Knoll Elementary School

**Ruthanne Kladder**
Oak Park Elementary School

**Bonnie Knapp**
West Junior High School

**Sue Laisure**
Sabin Elementary School

**Stan Malaski**
Oak Park Elementary School

**Jody Meyers**
Sabin Elementary School

**Marsha Myles**
East Junior High School

**Mary Beth O'Neil**
Traverse Heights Elementary School

**Jan Palkowski**
East Junior High School

**Karen Richardson**
Old Mission Elementary School

**Kristin Sak**
Bertha Vos Elementary School

**Mary Beth Schmitt**
East Junior High School

**Mike Schrotenboer**
Norris Elementary School

**Gail Smith**
Willow Hill Elementary School

**Karrie Tufts**
Eastern Elementary School

**Mike Wilson**
East Junior High School

**Tom Wilson**
West Junior High School

## Minnesota

*Minneapolis*

**Betsy Ford**
Northeast Middle School

## New York

*East Elmhurst*

**Allison Clark**
Louis Armstrong Middle School

**Dorothy Hershey**
Louis Armstrong Middle School

**J. Lewis McNeece**
Louis Armstrong Middle School

**Rossana Perez**
Louis Armstrong Middle School

**Merna Porter**
Louis Armstrong Middle School

**Marie Turini**
Louis Armstrong Middle School

## North Carolina

*Durham*

**Everly Broadway**
Durham Public Schools

**Thomas Carson**
Duke School for Children

**Mary Hebrank**
Duke School for Children

**Bill O'Connor**
Duke School for Children

**Ruth Pershing**
Duke School for Children

**Peter Reichert**
Duke School for Children

*Elizabeth City*

**Rita Banks**
Elizabeth City Middle School

**Beth Chaundry**
Elizabeth City Middle School

**Amy Cuthbertson**
Elizabeth City Middle School

**Deni Dennison**
Elizabeth City Middle School

**Jean Gray**
Elizabeth City Middle School

**John McMenamin**
Elizabeth City Middle School

**Nicollette Nixon**
Elizabeth City Middle School

**Malinda Norfleet**
Elizabeth City Middle School

**Joyce O'Neal**
Elizabeth City Middle School

**Clevie Sawyer**
Elizabeth City Middle School

**Juanita Shannon**
Elizabeth City Middle School

**Terry Thorne**
Elizabeth City Middle School

**Rebecca Wardour**
Elizabeth City Middle School

**Leora Winslow**
Elizabeth City Middle School

*Franklinton*

**Susan Haywood**
Franklinton Elementary School

**Clyde Melton**
Franklinton Elementary School

*Louisburg*

**Lisa Anderson**
Terrell Lane Middle School

**Jackie Frazier**
Terrell Lane Middle School

**Pam Harris**
Terrell Lane Middle School

## Ohio

*Toledo*

**Bonnie Bias**
Hawkins Elementary School

**Marsha Jackish**
Hawkins Elementary School

**Lee Jagodzinski**
DeVeaux Junior High School

**Norma J. King**
Old Orchard Elementary School

**Margaret McCready**
Old Orchard Elementary School

**Carmella Morton**
DeVeaux Junior High School

**Karen C. Rohrs**
Hawkins Elementary School

**Marie Sahloff**
DeVeaux Junior High School

**L. Michael Vince**
McTigue Junior High School

**Brenda D. Watkins**
Old Orchard Elementary School

## Oregon

*Portland*

**Roberta Cohen**
Catlin Gabel School

**David Ellenberg**
Catlin Gabel School

**Sara Normington**
Catlin Gabel School

**Karen Scholte-Arce**
Catlin Gabel School

*West Linn*

**Marge Burack**
Wood Middle School

**Tracy Wygant**
Athey Creek Middle School

*Canby*

**Sandra Kralovec**
Ackerman Middle School

## Pennsylvania

*Pittsburgh*

**Sheryl Adams**
Reizenstein Middle School

**Sue Barie**
Frick International Studies Academy

**Suzie Berry**
Frick International Studies Academy

**Richard Delgrosso**
Frick International Studies Academy

**Janet Falkowski**
Frick International Studies Academy

**Joanne George**
Reizenstein Middle School

**Harriet Hopper**
Reizenstein Middle School

**Chuck Jessen**
Reizenstein Middle School

**Ken Labuskes**
Reizenstein Middle School

**Barbara Lewis**
Reizenstein Middle School

**Sharon Mihalich**
Reizenstein Middle School

**Marianne O'Connor**
Frick International Studies Academy

**Mark Sammartino**
Reizenstein Middle School

## Washington

*Seattle*

**Chris Johnson**
University Preparatory Academy

**Rick Purn**
University Preparatory Academy

# Contents

**T**his is the first unit in the *Connected Mathematics*™ curriculum that will develop students' abilities to understand and reason about probability. Students will gain an understanding of experimental and theoretical probabilities and the relationship between them. The unit also makes important connections between probability and rational numbers, geometry, statistics, science, and business.

Questions about how likely an event is are asked every day. Such questions ask about the probability of an event happening, and the answers to them are important to many people, such as people planning picnics or playing sports and games, insurance-company employees, and health professionals. This unit explores different types of probability questions in contexts that are interesting to students in grade 6, such as games, advertising, contests, and the genetics of tongue curling.

Investigations 1, 2, and 3 focus on experimental probabilities and the idea of the chances that some event will occur. Students will have many opportunities to collect data through experimentation—using such things as coins, marshmallows, and spinners—and then use the data to assign experimental probabilities to the results. Investigations 4 and 5 formally introduce the terms *probability* and *theoretical probability*. The area represented on spinners, the sum of two number cubes, and colors of various objects drawn from a bag are analyzed both theoretically and experimentally. Investigations 6 and 7 give students opportunities to apply and further develop their knowledge about probability in a variety of interesting situations, including applications of probability in contests and genetics.

The terms *chance* and *probability* are applied to situations that have uncertain outcomes on individual trials but a regular pattern of outcomes over many trials. For example, when we toss a coin, we are uncertain whether it will come up heads or tails, but we do know that over the long run, if it is a fair coin, we will get about half heads and half tails. This does not mean we won't get several heads in a row, or that if we get heads now we are more likely to get tails on the next toss. This is a difficult concept for students to grasp: uncertainty on an individual outcome, but predictable regularity in the long run. It often takes a significant amount of time and a variety of experiences that challenge prior conceptions before students understand this basic concept of probability.

If we toss a tack into the air, we know that it will land on either its head or its side. However, if we toss the tack many times, we can use the ratio of the number of times it lands on its side to the total number of tosses to estimate the likelihood that the tack will land on its side. Since we find this ratio through experimentation, it is called an *experimental probability.*

Many uses of probability in daily life are based on experimental probabilities. We collect data for a large number of trials and observe the frequency of a particular result. This is the *relative-frequency interpretation* of probability. The probability that it will rain or that Shaquille O'Neal will make a free throw are two examples of experimental probabilities based on relative frequencies.

The experimental probability that a coin will land heads up can be expressed as:

$$P(head) = \frac{\text{number of times the coin lands heads up}}{\text{number of tosses}}$$

We can also determine the *theoretical probability* of a fair coin landing heads up or tails up by analyzing the situation. If we toss a fair coin, we know that it will land either heads up or tails up and that each outcome is *equally likely*. Since there are two possible equally likely outcomes, the probability of a fair coin landing heads up is 1 out of 2, or $\frac{1}{2}$. We can write this as P(head) $= \frac{1}{2}$. In general, the theoretical probability that a coin will land heads up can be expressed as:

$$P(head) = \frac{\text{number of favorable outcomes}}{\text{number of possible outcomes}} = \frac{1 \text{ (there is 1 head on a coin)}}{2 \text{(there are 2 possible outcomes)}}$$

Another example of a theoretical probability that occurs in this unit involves rolling a number cube. When a number cube is rolled, there are six possible outcomes: 1, 2, 3, 4, 5, and 6. Each outcome is equally likely on any roll of the number cube. Thus, $P(1) = P(2) = P(3) = P(4) = P(5) = P(6) = \frac{1}{6}$. We can use this theoretical probability to make an estimate: if a number cube is tossed many times, we expect each number to occur about $\frac{1}{6}$ of the time. We can also compute the probability of events that are made up of more than one equally likely outcome. For example, the theoretical probability of rolling a multiple of 3 on a number cube is $\frac{2}{6}$, since two of the six possible *equally likely* outcomes, 3 and 6, are multiples of 3.

In some situations it is easier to find theoretical probabilities, and in some it is easier to find experimental probabilities. For example, in this unit students will find experimental probabilities of a marshmallow landing on an end or a side when it is tossed, but they will not be able to determine the theoretical probabilities (because although "end" and "side" are the possible outcomes, they are not necessarily equally likely).

Probabilities are useful for predicting what will happen over the long run, yet a theoretical or experimental probability does not tell us exactly what will happen. For example, if we toss a coin 40 times, we may not get exactly 20 heads; but if we toss a coin 1000 times, the fraction of heads will be fairly close to $\frac{1}{2}$. Experimental data gathered over many trials should produce probabilities that are close to the theoretical probabilities (this idea is sometimes called the Law of Large Numbers). If we can calculate a theoretical probability, we can use it to predict what will happen in the long run rather than having to rely on experimentation.

Once we have a probability—theoretical or experimental—we can use it to make predictions. For example, if a coin is tossed 1000 times, we would predict that a head will occur about 500 times. If a number cube is rolled 1000 times, we would predict that a 3 will occur about $\frac{1}{6}$ of the time or about 167 times.

It is important for students to realize that a small amount of data may produce wide variation among samples and that only over many trials can we make good estimates for what will happen in the long run. In other words, for our experimental probabilities to be good estimates of the theoretical probabilities, we must base our experimental probabilities on many trials.

**H**ow Likely Is It? **was created to help students**

- Become acquainted with probability informally through experiments

- Understand that probabilities are useful for predicting what will happen over the long run

- Understand that probabilities are useful for making decisions

- Understand that there are two ways to obtain probabilities: by gathering data from experiments (experimental probability) and by analyzing the possible equally likely outcomes (theoretical probability)

- Understand the concepts of equally likely and unequally likely

- Understand the relationship between experimental and theoretical probabilities: experimental probabilities are better estimates of theoretical probabilities when they are based on larger numbers of trials

- Determine and critically interpret statements of probability

- Develop strategies for finding both experimental and theoretical probabilities

- Organize data into lists or charts of equally likely outcomes as a strategy for finding theoretical probabilities (other strategies, such as tree diagrams and the area model, will be introduced in the grade 7 probability unit, *What Do You Expect?*)

- Use graphs and tallies to summarize and display data

- Use data displayed in graphs and tallies to find experimental probabilities

The overall goal of Connected Mathematics is to help students develop sound mathematical habits. Through their work in this and other data units, students learn important questions to ask themselves about any situation that can be represented and modeled mathematically, such as: *What makes an event uncertain? How can we get useful information about such uncertain events? What do we mean by "predictable"? When can a series of uncertain events become predictable? Why is probability a mathematics topic? How can we use mathematics to identify how probable an event may be? What probability is associated with an event that is certain? With an event that could never happen? What kinds of experiments can be performed to find the probability of an event? Can we find a way to compare a probability found mathematically with a probability found experimentally?*

### Investigation 1: A First Look at Chance

Students flip a coin 30 times and then compute the experimental probability of a head occurring on a toss of a coin—first by using only their own data and then by using the entire class's data. To get an even larger set of data, a computer (if available) is used to generate data and produce a graph of the fraction of tosses that result in heads. The graph is used to help students begin to understand the long-term regularity in the behavior of coins. The phrase *equally likely* is introduced, and students are asked to decide whether various events are equally likely.

### Investigation 2: More Experiments with Chance

Students experiment with marshmallows, finding the experimental probabilities that each of two sizes of marshmallow will land on an end or a side. Individual groups' data are combined to produce a larger set of data so students get a better estimate of how the marshmallows will behave over the long run.

### Investigation 3: Using Spinners to Predict Chances

The pattern of collecting data, analyzing data, and making predictions continues in this investigation. The emphasis is on experimental data, but students can determine what fraction of the total area of a spinner each section makes up. If a large amount of data is collected, the fractions that were determined experimentally should be fairly close to the fractions represented by the spinner (the theoretical probabilities). Though students are comparing theoretical and experimental probabilities, the words are not introduced until Investigation 4.

### Investigation 4: Theoretical Probabilities

Probability is formally introduced in a game-show setting, in which players need to determine the probability of drawing a certain color of block from a container in which the total number of each color and the total number of blocks is unknown. This whole-class activity is used to form a working definition of *probability* and to emphasize specific characteristics of probability: that the sum of the probabilities of all outcomes is 1; that probability is a number from 0 to 1; and that a probability of 0 or 1 has a particular significance. Students are asked to make comparisons between experimental and theoretical probabilities, and they have their first experience with making an organized list to find theoretical probabilities.

### Investigation 5: Analyzing Games of Chance

Students play and analyze a game that involves arranging 12 markers in columns numbered 1 through 12. A pair of number cubes is rolled, and a marker is removed from the column whose number matches the sum of the numbers on the cubes. The first team to remove all their markers wins the game. After playing the game, students list the possible outcomes of a roll of a pair of number cubes and use this information to map out winning strategies for the game.

### Investigation 6: More About Games of Chance

Students design a simulation to find an experimental probability of winning a prize in a promotional contest involving scratch-off game cards. They are also asked to find the theoretical probability of winning by making an organized list of the possible pairs of spots that could be scratched off. The ACE questions continue the theme of promotions and are designed to help students realize that there are many loopholes in advertising claims and contests.

## Investigation 7: Probability and Genetics

This investigation introduces biology as a source of applications for probability. Students determine how many students in their class can curl their tongues and use this data to make predictions about the probability of any one person being able to curl his or her tongue. This experimental method is compared with the way in which geneticists predict the traits of children by examining the genetic makeup of the parents. Students then gain experience with determining whether a person will have the tongue-curling trait based on genetic probabilities. In the ACE questions, students determine eye color based on genetics and probability.

## Connections to Other Units

The ideas in *How Likely Is It?* build on and connect to several big ideas in other Connected Mathematics units.

| Big Idea | Prior Work | Future Work |
|---|---|---|
| developing understanding of probability | performing operations with whole numbers; finding factors and multiples (*Prime Time*); developing understanding of ratio in fraction, percent, or decimal form (*Bits and Pieces I*) | applying rational numbers (*Bits and Pieces II, Comparing and Scaling*); finding probabilities and expected values for more complex games and situations (*What Do You Expect?*); using probabilities to make inferences and predictions (*Samples and Populations*); developing counting strategies to help determine probabilities (*Clever Counting*) |
| determining experimental probabilities | collecting and organizing data (*Data About Us*); working with ratio and proportion (*Bits and Pieces I*) | collecting and organizing data from complex games and situations to determine experimental probabilities (*What Do You Expect?*); using experimental probabilities to make inferences and predictions (*Samples and Populations, Clever Counting*) |
| determining theoretical probabilities | analyzing games or situations (*Prime Time*); identifying and organizing all possible outcomes and looking for patterns (*Data About Us, Covering and Surrounding*); working with ratio and proportion (*Bits and Pieces I*) | devising strategies for finding and applying theoretical probabilities (*What Do You Expect?*); making inferences and predictions using theoretical probabilities (*Samples and Populations*); developing of counting strategies to determine theoretical probabilities (*Clever Counting*) |
| developing understanding of randomness | identifying and organizing all possible outcomes of a game or situation and looking for patterns (*Data About Us, Covering and Surrounding*); working with ratio and proportion (*Bits and Pieces I*) | analyzing and comparing games and situations in which outcomes are random or biased (*What Do You Expect?*); selecting and analyzing random samples to make inferences and predictions about a larger population (*Samples and Populations*) |

## Materials

### For students

- Labsheets
- Calculators
- Pennies (3 per pair or group)
- Number cubes (1 per pair)
- Large and small marshmallows (10 of each size per pair or group)
- Bobby pins or paper clips (for making spinners; 1 per pair or group)
- Game markers, such as counters, buttons, or other small objects (12 per pair)
- Game chips (3 per student; for the Quiz and the Unit Test)
- Materials for simulating the contest in Problem 6.1, such as blocks, spinners, and sheets of card stock
- Paper cups (optional; 1 per pair or group)
- Computer and the Coin Game program (optional; see "Technology" below)
- Blocks or other objects (optional; in 3 colors)
- Opaque bucket or bag (optional; 2 per group)

### For the teacher

- Transparencies and transparency markers (optional)
- Opaque bucket or bag filled with 9 red blocks, 6 yellow blocks, and 3 blue blocks (substitute other objects or colors if necessary)
- Second opaque bucket or bag (optional for Problem 4.3)
- Small prizes (optional)
- Number cubes (2 cubes of different colors; optional)
- Scratch-off game card (optional)

## Technology

Connected Mathematics was developed with the belief that calculators should always be available and that students should decide when to use them. For this reason, we do not designate specific problems as "calculator problems."

The optional Coin Game program may be used with Problem 1.1. This program generates coin tosses and graphs the percent of heads versus the number of trials. It allows you to generate large numbers of coin-tosses and to help your students see how the fraction of heads levels off near $\frac{1}{2}$ after a large number of tosses. This program can be downloaded from the Connected Mathematics web site (http://www.ns.msu.edu/CMP/cmp.html), or it can be obtained by sending $10 (to cover the cost of the disk, the documentation, and shipping and handling) to: Connected Education Technology, P.O. Box 1014, East Lansing, MI 48826. Please indicate whether you would like the Windows or Macintosh version.

## Resources

*For students*

For more information about genetics and probability, you and your students will enjoy this interesting book:

Gonick, Larry, and Mark Wheelis. *Cartoon Guide to Genetics.* New York: Barnes and Noble, 1983.

*For teachers*

If you would like information on more probability and statistics topics of interest to students, try these books:

Shapiro, Andrew. *We're Number One.* New York: Vintage Books, 1992.

Shook, Michael D., and Robert L. Shook. *The Book of Odds.* New York: Penguin Books, 1991.

## Pacing Chart

This pacing chart gives estimates of the class time required for each investigation and assessment piece. Shaded rows indicate opportunities for assessment.

| Investigations and Assessments | Class Time |
|---|---|
| **1** A First Look at Chance | 2 days |
| **2** More Experiments with Chance | 2 days |
| **3** Using Spinners to Predict Chances | 2 days |
| Quiz | 1 day |
| Check-Up 1 | 1 day |
| **4** Theoretical Probabilities | 3 days |
| **5** Analyzing Games of Chance | 2 days |
| **6** More About Games of Chance | 2 days |
| **7** Probability and Genetics | 3 days |
| Check-Up 2 | $\frac{1}{2}$ day |
| Self-Assessment | Take home |
| Unit Test | 1 day |

# Vocabulary

The following words and concepts are introduced and used in *How Likely Is It?* Concepts in the left column are essential for student understanding of this and future units. The Descriptive Glossary gives descriptions of many of these and other words used in *How Likely Is It?*

| **Essential** | **Nonessential** |
|---|---|
| certain event | fair (as in fair game, fair coin) |
| chances | favorable outcome |
| equally likely events | possible |
| event | probable |
| experimental probability | random events |
| impossible event | trial |
| outcome | |
| probability | |
| theoretical probability | |

# Assessment Summary

### Embedded Assessment

Opportunities for informal assessment of student progress are embedded throughout *How Likely Is It?* in the problems, the ACE questions, and the Mathematical Reflections. Suggestions for observing as students discover and explore mathematical ideas, for probing to guide their progress in developing concepts and skills, and for questioning to determine their level of understanding can be found in the *Launch, Explore,* or *Summarize* sections of all investigation problems. Some examples:

- Investigation 2, Problem 2.2 *Launch* (page 21b) suggests a way you can assess whether your students understand the difference between possible and probable.
- Investigation 4, Problem 4.3 *Explore* (page 41c) suggests how you can help your students organize all the possible outcomes of an experiment.
- Investigation 1, Problem 1.1 *Summarize* (page 13b) suggests ways that you can help your students see that, over the long run, the percent of coins that land heads up when tossed is very close to $\frac{1}{2}$.

### ACE Assignments

An ACE (Applications—Connections—Extensions) section appears at the end of each investigation. To help you assign ACE questions, a list of assignment choices is given in the margin next to the reduced student page for each problem. Each list indicates the ACE questions that students should be able to answer after they complete the problem.

### Partner Quiz

One quiz, which may be given after Investigation 3, is provided with *How Likely Is It?* This quiz is designed to be completed by pairs of students with the opportunity for revision based on teacher feedback. You will find the quiz and its answer key in the Assessment Resources section. As an alternative to the quiz provided, you can construct your own quiz by combining questions from the Question Bank, the quiz, and unassigned ACE questions.

## Check-Ups

Two check-ups, which may be given after Investigations 3 and 7, are provided for use as quick quizzes or warm-up activities. Check-ups are designed for students to complete individually. You will find the check-ups and their answer keys in the Assessment Resources section.

## Question Bank

A Question Bank provides questions you can use for homework, reviews, or quizzes. You will find the Question Bank and its answer key in the Assessment Resources section.

## Notebook/Journal

Students should have notebooks to record and organize their work. In the notebooks will be their journals along with sections for vocabulary, homework, and quizzes and check-ups. In their journals, students can take notes, solve investigation problems, and record their mathematical reflections. You should assess student journals for completeness rather than correctness; journals should be seen as "safe" places where students can try out their thinking. A Notebook Checklist and a Self-Assessment are provided in the Assessment Resources section. The Notebook Checklist helps students organize their notebooks. The Self-Assessment guides students as they review their notebooks to determine which ideas they have mastered and which ideas they still need to work on.

## The Unit Test

The final assessment in *How Likely Is It?* is a test. The test focuses on three situations: a game, drawing marbles from a bag, and a gumball machine. Several questions are asked about each situation. Some of these questions check the understanding of fundamental concepts. Others are problem-solving questions that probe more deeply to see how students reason about what they know.

## Introducing Your Students to *How Likely Is It?*

**T**o launch the unit, you might begin by discussing the probability examples on the opening page of the student edition. Encourage students to share their ideas about where probability might be useful to them.

Ask students how probability might help them make decisions in their lives.

Ask students what they think the word *probability* (or the *chances* that something will occur) means. Don't look for "correct" answers at this time. Do, however, present an opportunity for the class to discuss the questions and to start to think about probabilities and what kinds of probabilities are needed to answer the questions. You may want to revisit these questions as students learn mathematical ideas and techniques that will help them to answer such questions.

# How Likely Is It?

*Imagine that you are one of four contestants on a game show. The host is holding a bucket containing red, yellow, and blue blocks. You cannot see the blocks. Each contestant guesses a color and then draws a block from the bucket. A contestant who correctly predicts the color of the block wins $500. After each draw, the block is returned to the bucket. What are your chances of winning the game? Is there an advantage to choosing first? Is there an advantage to choosing last?*

*Suppose you have a scratch-off game card with five spots. Each spot covers the name of a prize. The names under two of the spots match. You are allowed to scratch off two spots. If the names under the spots match, you win the prize. How likely is it that you will win?*

*Some people can curl their tongues into a U shape; other people can't. What are the chances that a person can curl her or his tongue?*

**H**ow do you make decisions? If you are deciding whether or not to carry an umbrella to school, you might ask yourself, "How likely is it that it will rain today?" If you are deciding whether to buy a lottery ticket, you might ask yourself, "What are the chances that I will win the lottery?" These questions are asking about the *probability* that a particular event will occur.

Determining probabilities can help you understand past events and make decisions about future events. In this unit, you will look at many questions that involve probability, including the three questions on the opposite page.

# Mathematical Highlights

**T**he Mathematical Highlights page provides information to students and to parents and other family members. It gives students a preview of the activities and problems in *How Likely Is It?* As they work through the unit, students can refer back to the Mathematical Highlights page to review what they have learned and to preview what is still to come. This page also tells students' families what mathematical ideas and activities will be covered as the class works through *How Likely Is It?*

## Mathematical Highlights

**I**n *How Likely Is It?*, you will explore concepts related to *chance* and *probability* applied to situations that have uncertain outcomes. This unit will help you to

● Become acquainted with probability through experiments;

● Understand the concepts of equally likely and not equally likely;

● Understand that there are two ways to build probability models: by gathering data from experiments (experimental probability) and by analyzing the possible equally likely outcomes (theoretical probability);

● Develop strategies for finding both experimental and theoretical probabilities;

● Understand that experimental probabilities are better estimates of theoretical probabilities when they are based on larger numbers of trials;

● Understand that probabilities are useful for predicting what will happen over the long run; and

● Determine and critically interpret statements of probability.

As you work on the problems of this unit, make it a habit to ask questions about situations that involve probability and uncertainty: *What are the possible outcomes that can occur for the event in this situation? How could I determine the experimental probability of each of the outcomes? Is it possible to determine the theoretical experimental probability of each of the outcomes? If so, what are these probabilities? How can I use the probabilities I have found to answer questions or make decisions about this situation?*

## The Investigations

The teaching materials for each investigation consist of three parts: an overview, student pages with teaching outlines, and detailed notes for teaching the investigation.

The overview of each investigation includes brief descriptions of the problems, the mathematical and problem-solving goals of the investigation, and a list of necessary materials.

Essential information for teaching the investigation is provided in the margins around the student pages. The "At a Glance" overviews are brief outlines of the Launch, Explore, and Summarize phases of each problem for reference as you work with the class. To help you assign homework, a list of "Assignment Choices" is provided next to each problem. Wherever space permits, answers to problems, follow-ups, ACE questions, and Mathematical Reflections appear next to the appropriate student pages.

The Teaching the Investigation section follows the student pages and is the heart of the Connected Mathematics curriculum. This section describes in detail the Launch, Explore, and Summarize phases for each problem. It includes all the information needed for teaching, along with suggestions for what you might say at key points in the teaching. Use this section to prepare lessons and as a guide for teaching an investigation.

## Assessment Resources

The Assessment Resources section contains blackline masters and answer keys for the quiz, check-ups, the Question Bank, and the Unit Test. Blackline masters for the Notebook Checklist and the Self-Assessment are given. These instruments support student self-evaluation, an important aspect of assessment in the *Connected Mathematics* curriculum.

## Blackline Masters

The Blackline Masters section includes masters for all labsheets and transparencies.

## Additional Practice

Practice pages for each investigation offer additional problems for students who need more practice with the basic concepts developed in the investigations as well as some continual review of earlier concepts.

## Descriptive Glossary

The Descriptive Glossary provides descriptions and examples of the key concepts in *How Likely Is It?* These descriptions are not intended to be formal definitions, but are meant to give you an idea of how students might make sense of these important concepts.

# A First Look at Chance

**T**his investigation introduces students to experimental probabilities.

In Problem 1.1, Flipping for Breakfast, students experiment to see for themselves that, over the long run, the fraction of heads that occurs when a coin is tossed—the experimental probability—is close to $\frac{1}{2}$. This result is what students expect, since they know instinctively that there are two equally likely outcomes. They may be able to predict ahead of time that if a coin is flipped 30 times, heads will result about 15 times. However, the main objective is for them to observe the variation in results with small numbers of trials and what happens as more data are added: they pool their data and discover that as the number of trials increases, the fraction of heads starts to level off near $\frac{1}{2}$. Problem 1.2, Analyzing Events, asks students to determine whether the possible resulting events of several given actions are equally likely.

## Mathematical and Problem-Solving Goals

- **To build intuition that probability, or chance, has to do with events that are uncertain but that have a pattern of regularity over the long run**

- **To determine relative frequencies from experimental data and use them to predict behavior over the long run**

- **To observe that small numbers of trials may produce wide variation in results**

- **To display collected data in graphs or tallies and use them to find experimental probabilities**

- **To recognize equally likely events**

| Materials | | |
|---|---|---|
| **Problem** | **For students** | **For the teacher** |
| **All** | Calculators | Transparencies 1.1 and 1.2 (optional) |
| **1.1** | Labsheets 1.1A and 1.1B (1 each per group), pennies (1 per group), paper cup (optional, 1 per group) | A computer and the Coin Game (optional); see "Technology" on page 1g for more information |

**Student Pages 5–13**     **Teaching the Investigation 13a–13e**

# A First Look at Chance

**O**ne way to make a decision about something is to do an experiment to see what is likely to happen. In this investigation, you will experiment with flipping a coin.

### 1.1 Flipping for Breakfast

Kalvin, an eighth grader, always has cereal for breakfast. He likes Cocoa Blast cereal so much that he wants to eat it every morning. Kalvin's mother wants him to eat Health Nut Flakes at least some mornings because it is more nutritious than Cocoa Blast.

Kalvin and his mother have come up with a fun way to determine which cereal Kalvin will have for breakfast. Each morning, Kalvin flips a coin. If the coin comes up heads, he will have Cocoa Blast. If he flips a tail, he will have Health Nut Flakes.

## Flipping for Breakfast

**Grouping:
Pairs or Small Groups**

### Launch
- Introduce Kalvin's breakfast-cereal problem.
- Discuss ways to prevent introducing systematic bias into the data collection.

### Explore
- As you circulate, check on flipping and tallying techniques.

### Summarize
- As a class, combine all the data collected in a table, first as individual entries and then as a running total.
- Ask about variation among groups.
- Ask which is more predictive—the data of individual groups or the combined class data.

### Assignment Choices
ACE questions 1–5 and 15 (give students several days to work on 15)

## Problem 1.1

How many days in June do you think Kalvin will eat Cocoa Blast?

Explore this question by flipping a coin 30 times to determine Kalvin's cereal for each morning in June. Use Labsheet 1.1 to help you collect your data.

### June

|    |    |    |    |    |    |
|----|----|----|----|----|----|
| 1  | 2  | 3  | 4  | 5  | 6  |
| 7  | 8  | 9  | 10 | 11 | 12 | 13 |
| 14 | 15 | 16 | 17 | 18 | 19 | 20 |
| 21 | 22 | 23 | 24 | 25 | 26 | 27 |
| 28 | 29 | 30 |    |    |    |    |

For each day, record the result of the flip (H or T) and the percent of heads so far. Use the data to make a coordinate graph with the days from 1 to 30 on the *x*-axis and the percent of heads so far on the *y*-axis.

### Problem 1.1 Follow-Up

Work with your teacher to combine the results from all the groups.

**1. a.** What fraction of the entire class's flips were heads?
   **b.** As you added more and more data, did the fraction of heads get closer to or further from $\frac{1}{2}$?
**2. a.** Based on what you found for June, how many times would you expect Kalvin to eat Cocoa Blast cereal in July?
   **b.** How many times would you expect Kalvin to eat Cocoa Blast cereal in a year?
**3.** Kalvin's mother told him that the chances of getting a head when you flip a coin are $\frac{1}{2}$. Does this mean that every time you flip a coin twice you will get one head and one tail? Explain your reasoning.

## Answers to Problem 1.1

Answers will vary. After conducting the experiment and discussing the follow-up questions, students should predict that Kalvin will eat Cocoa Blast cereal about 15 of the 30 days of June.

## Answers to Problem 1.1 Follow-Up

1. a. Results will vary but should be close to $\frac{1}{2}$.

   b. Results will vary, but students should find that as more trials are added, the fraction of tosses that are heads levels off at around $\frac{1}{2}$.

2. a. Kalvin will eat Cocoa Blast about half the time, or about 15 days of the 31 days in July.

   b. Over a year, or 365 days, Kalvin will eat Cocoa Blast about 180 mornings.

3. See page 13d.

## 1.2 Analyzing Events

Kalvin found a penny near a railroad track. It looked flattened and a bit bent, so Kalvin assumed it must have been run over by a train. He decided to use this unusual penny for determining his breakfast.

Kalvin's mother became suspicious of the penny at the end of June because Kalvin had eaten Health Nut Flakes only seven times. She explained why she was suspicious. "With a fair coin, heads and tails are **equally likely** results. This means that you have the same chance of getting a head as a tail. I just don't think your coin is fair!"

### Think about this!

**D**o you think heads and tails are equally likely with Kalvin's penny? How could Kalvin find out whether his coin is fair?

Kalvin was not quite sure what his mother meant by *equally likely,* so she made up an example to help explain it.

"Suppose everyone in our family wrote his or her name on a card and put the card in a hat. If you mixed up the cards and pulled one out, each name would have an equally likely chance of being picked. But suppose I put my name in the hat ten times. Then when you picked one card out of the hat, our names wouldn't all have an equal chance of being picked—my name would have a greater chance of being chosen than everyone else's name."

**Investigation 1: A First Look at Chance** | **7**

### Launch

- Talk about the meaning of *equally likely.*

- Make sure students understand what they are to do.

### Explore

- Have students individually consider the problems and then discuss them in groups or pairs.

- As you circulate, listen to students' reasoning.

- Have groups work on the follow-up.

### Summarize

- As a class, discuss each action and whether the possible resulting events are equally likely.

- Have groups share their answers to the follow-up.

## Tips for the Linguistically Diverse Classroom

**Rebus Scenario** The Rebus Scenario technique is described in detail in *Getting to Know Connected Mathematics.* This technique involves sketching rebuses on the chalkboard that correspond to key words in the story or information you present orally. Example: some key words and phrases for which you may need to draw rebuses while discussing the material on this page: *Kalvin* (a stick figure of a boy), *penny* (a coin), *railroad track* (a track), *bent* (the coin now bent), *mother* (a stick figure of a woman), *Health Nut Flakes* (a box of cereal), *card* (a card), *hat* (a hat).

## Assignment Choices

ACE questions 6–14 and unassigned choices from the previous problem

### Problem 1.2

In A–H, decide whether the possible resulting events of each action are equally likely, and briefly explain your answer.

| Action | Possible resulting events |
|---|---|
| **A.** You toss a soda can. | The can lands on its side, the can lands upside down, or the can lands right side up. |
| **B.** You roll a number cube. | 1, 2, 3, 4, 5, or 6 |
| **C.** You check the weather in Alaska on a December day. | It snows, it rains, or it does not rain or snow. |
| **D.** The Pittsburgh Steelers play a football game. | The Steelers win, the Steelers lose, or the Steelers tie. |
| **E.** A baby is born. | The baby is a boy or the baby is a girl. |
| **F.** A baby is born. | The baby is right-handed or the baby is left-handed. |
| **G.** You guess on a true/false question. | The answer is right or the answer is wrong. |
| **H.** You shoot a free throw. | You make the basket or you miss. |

■ **Problem 1.2 Follow-Up**

**1.** Describe three other situations in which the possible resulting events are equally likely.

**2.** Describe three other situations in which the possible resulting events are not equally likely.

## Answers to Problem 1.2

A. The events are not equally likely. A soda can is more likely to land on its side than on either of its ends.

B. The events are equally likely. The six sides of a fair number cube have the same chance of landing on top.

C. The events are probably not equally likely. Snow is probably more likely than rain.

D–H.   See page 13d.

## Answers to Problem 1.2 Follow-Up

Answers will vary.

As you work on these ACE questions, use your calculator whenever you need it.

# Applications

**1. a.** Sarah flipped a coin 50 times, and heads turned up 28 times. What fraction of the 50 flips of the coin turned up heads?

   **b.** If the coin is fair, and Sarah flips it 500 times, how many times should she expect it to come up heads?

**2.** Suppose Kalvin flipped a coin to determine his breakfast cereal every day starting on his twelfth birthday and continuing until his eighteenth birthday. How many times would you expect him to eat Cocoa Blast cereal?

**3.** Kalvin flipped a coin five days in a row and got tails every time. He told his mother there must be something wrong with the coin he was using. Do you think there is something wrong with the coin? How could Kalvin find out?

**4.** Len flipped a coin three times and got a head each time. What are the chances he will get a tail on his next toss? Explain your reasoning.

**5.** Is it possible to flip a coin 20 times and have it turn up heads 20 times? Is this likely to happen? Explain your reasoning.

## Answers

### Applications

**1a.** $\frac{28}{50} = \frac{14}{25}$

**1b.** about 250

**2.** There are about 6 years × 365 days = 2190 (or 2191 or 2192; some students might add a day or two for leap years) days for which Kalvin will flip a coin. We would expect him to flip heads and eat Cocoa Blast about half of those days, or about 1095 days.

**3.** With only five trials, we cannot be certain. Kalvin should flip the coin many more times if he wants to find out whether the coin is fair or not.

**4.** The chances are $\frac{1}{2}$ or 50%. This is confusing for students, because they expect the average to be about 50% in the long run. If a coin turns up heads three times in a row, it is *not* more likely to turn up tails the next time.

**5.** See page 13e.

## Connections

**6.** The events are probably not equally likely. It is more likely that a friend or family member would call than a stranger.

**7.** The events are probably not equally likely. Students will probably have a good idea of whether the local temperature is more likely to be over or under 30° F.

**8.** The events are equally likely, because each of the three patterns takes up a third of the circle's area in pie-shaped wedges. Students may want to analyze this spinner with their angle rulers or experiment with this spinner.

**9.** These events are not equally likely, since the teacher nearly always arrives on time.

**10.** The events are probably not equally likely, as the size and layout of the town or city would affect the number of accidents. (To find out for your city, you would need to know the average number of accidents that occur on a given day; the average might be different for a Monday than a Saturday.)

# Connections

In 6–10, decide whether the resulting events are equally likely, and briefly explain your answer.

| Action | Possible resulting events |
|---|---|
| **6.** Your phone rings at 9:00 P.M. | The caller is your best friend, the caller is a relative, or the caller is someone else. |
| **7.** You check the temperature in your area tomorrow. | The temperature is over 30°F or the temperature is under 30° F. |
| **8.** You spin this spinner. | The spinner lands on stripes, the spinner lands on hearts, or the spinner lands on dots. |
| **9.** Your teacher arrives at school in the morning. | Your teacher arrives on time or your teacher is late. |
| **10.** You find out how many car accidents occurred in your city or town yesterday. | There were fewer than five accidents, there were exactly five accidents, or there were more than five accidents. |

In 11–14, use this graph, which shows the average number of tornadoes per year in several states:

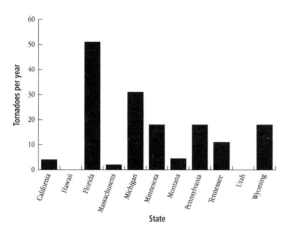

11. Is it equally likely for a tornado to hit somewhere in California as for a tornado to hit somewhere in Florida?

12. Is it equally likely for a tornado to hit somewhere in Minnesota as for a tornado to hit somewhere in Pennsylvania?

13. Is it equally likely for a tornado to hit somewhere in Massachusetts as for a tornado to hit somewhere in California?

14. Based on these data, is a person living in Montana in more danger of being hit by a tornado than a person living in Massachusetts? Explain your reasoning.

**11.** no; A tornado is more likely to hit somewhere in Florida.

**12.** yes

**13.** no; A tornado is more likely to hit somewhere in California.

**14.** no; Although the data show that more tornadoes strike Montana than Massachusetts, this does not mean that a resident of Montana is more likely to be hit than a resident of Massachusetts. For example, consider that Massachusetts is much, much smaller than Montana.

## Extensions

**15.** There are ten possibilities in all:

HHTTT

HTHTT    THHTT

HTTHT    THTHT    TTHHT

HTTTH    THTTH    TTHTH    TTTHH

Possible explanation: I have organized my list in a way that helps me be sure I have all the possibilities. First I put one H in the first position and moved the second H through the other four positions. Then I put the first H in the second position and moved the other H through the third, fourth, and fifth positions. I continued this pattern until I'd covered all the possibilities. I know I haven't duplicated any because the first H changes position with each column.

## Extensions

**15.** Monday was the first day Kalvin flipped a coin to determine his cereal. During his first five days of flipping, he only had Cocoa Blast twice. One way that Kalvin could have done this was to have flipped heads on Monday and Tuesday and tails on Wednesday, Thursday, and Friday. We can write this as:

| Monday | Tuesday | Wednesday | Thursday | Friday |
|--------|---------|-----------|----------|--------|
| H | H | T | T | T |

Find every other way Kalvin could have flipped the coin during the week and had Cocoa Blast cereal twice. Explain how you know that you have found every way.

# Mathematical Reflections

In this investigation, you experimented with coins to determine the fraction of heads and tails that occurred when you tossed a coin 30 times and when you combined the tosses from all the students in your class. You also investigated other situations to evaluate whether the possible resulting events were equally likely. These questions will help you summarize what you have learned:

**1** What does it mean to say that the chances of getting a head when a coin is tossed are $\frac{1}{2}$?

**2** If you experiment by tossing a coin and tallying the results, are 30 tosses as good as 500 tosses to predict the chances of a coin landing tails up? Explain why or why not.

**3** **a.** What does it mean for the results of some action to be equally likely?

**b.** Give an example of an action in which the possible resulting events are equally likely.

**c.** Give an example of an action in which the possible resulting events are not equally likely.

**4** If you toss a fair coin, is it *possible* to get 25 heads in a row? Is this *likely* to happen?

Think about your answers to these questions, discuss your ideas with other students and your teacher, and then write a summary of your findings in your journal.

## Possible Answers

**1.** It means that over many trials the coin will land on heads or tails about an equal number of times. It also means that the chances of a head or a tail on an individual toss are the same. It does not mean that in 10 tosses you are guaranteed 5 heads. It is *possible* to get 5 heads, but it is not a sure thing. However, in 5000 tosses you expect to get *about* 2500 heads.

**2.** 30 trials will not give you enough data to make a good prediction. There is usually wide variability in samples based on small numbers of trials. However, as the number of trials increases, the variability decreases. Two sets of 500 trials are much more likely to give similar results than two sets of 30 trials.

**3a.** Each event will happen about the same number of times over the long run. The chances of each event happening are the same.

**3b.** In the drawing for the Michigan Lottery grand prize, each ticket is equally likely to be drawn from the barrel.

**3c.** If a professional basketball player and his 10-year-old brother each shoot a free throw, the professional basketball player is more likely to make the basket.

**4.** It is *possible*. However, it is very *unlikely* that heads will happen 25 times in a row.

# TEACHING THE INVESTIGATION

## 1.1 • Flipping for Breakfast

In this problem, students collect the results of coin tosses and use the data to determine the chances of tossing a head. They know intuitively that the probability is $\frac{1}{2}$, and through their experimentation they discover that although there is a great deal of variation for a small number of trials, the fraction of heads for a large number of trials is close to $\frac{1}{2}$.

### Launch

Introduce the problem by telling Kalvin's story and reading the question posed in the problem. An effective technique is to have students predict, before they conduct the experiment, how many days in June Kalvin will have Cocoablast for breakfast. Making predictions will give them a stake in the results and help to ensure that they are focused on the question.

Next, discuss the need for students to make sure that the way they conduct the experiment won't affect—or *bias*—the outcome.

> What kinds of things could happen to affect the data you gather in this problem?
>
> How should you flip a penny to be sure you have a fair trial?

Talk to the class about *systematic bias,* the introduction of bias through nonrandom ways of generating the data, such as always starting with tails facing up when tossing a coin. Discuss how systematic bias can affect what is learned from an experiment. Data collected in a random way can help us to better predict what to expect when a coin is tossed.

Perhaps the class can decide on a coin-tossing technique that helps ensure the results are random. For example, students might decide to shake the coin in a cup and then spill it onto their desks. At this stage, *random* means there is no systematic bias in the data—that is, the coin's behavior is not affected in a predictable way by how it is tossed.

Have students work in pairs or small groups. Distribute Labsheet 1.1A to each group. This labsheet shows a calendar for the month of June. Explain that students are to toss a penny once for each day and record the result, H or T, in the appropriate day.

After each toss, students should fill in the table below the calendar to show the number and percent of heads that have occurred so far. The table will help students organize the results so they can easily form fractions—which they can interpret as percents—showing the relative frequencies of occurrence of heads:

$$P(H) = \frac{\text{number of times a head occurred}}{\text{total number of flips}}$$

Students can compute the fraction of heads after any number of trials by dividing the number of heads that occurred to that point by the date (which is the number of trials). When students understand how to record their data, remind them of the problem they are trying to solve and let them get to work.

## Explore

As students work, check the way they are tossing the coins to make sure they are not introducing bias. Check to see that they are recording their data and calculating the percents correctly. After students have collected the data and calculated the percents, give each group a copy of Labsheet 1.1B and ask them to plot their results on the axes given.

## Summarize

Facilitate the combining of the class's data. Ask one group at a time to report how many heads they flipped in 30 trials, and record the result in a table; for example:

| Number of heads | Fraction | Percent |
|---|---|---|
| 10 | $\frac{10}{30}$ or $\frac{1}{3}$ | about 33.3% |
| 19 | $\frac{19}{30}$ | about 63.3% |
| 15 | $\frac{15}{30}$ or $\frac{1}{2}$ | 50% |
| 13 | $\frac{13}{30}$ | about 43.3% |

The number of heads for each group will probably vary considerably, with some results far from 50%. You may also want to make a line plot with the possible number of heads—from 1 through 30—along the horizontal axis.

After you have collected all the data, combine it by making another table showing a running total of the number of trials and number of heads. Add the data for one group at a time, recomputing the fraction and percent of heads each time.

| Total number of trials | Total number of heads | Fraction | Percent |
|---|---|---|---|
| 30 | 10 | $\frac{10}{30}$ or $\frac{1}{3}$ | about 33.3% |
| 60 | 29 | $\frac{29}{60}$ | about 48.3% |
| 90 | 44 | $\frac{44}{90}$ | about 49% |
| 120 | 57 | $\frac{57}{120}$ | 47.5% |

As more data are added, the fraction of heads will begin to level off near $\frac{1}{2}$. It is important for students to recognize that as the number of trials increases, the fraction of heads gets closer to $\frac{1}{2}$, which is what they would expect from their previous experience with coin tossing.

Use the data from this table to make a coordinate graph, similar to the graphs students made on Labsheet 1.1B, of the number of trials versus the percent of heads.

If you have the CMP Coin Game, ask students whether they think the fraction of heads would be closer to or further away from $\frac{1}{2}$ if a computer ran many more trials than were run in class. Run the computer program with the students, or run it yourself before class and show them the results. If students have access to computers outside of your class, you might make copies of the program for them to try on their own. The program asks how many trials you would like to run and then graphs the results of that number of flips. The graph should level off to about $\frac{1}{2}$ over hundreds of trials. For example, with 100 trials, the graph might look something like the graph shown on the next page.

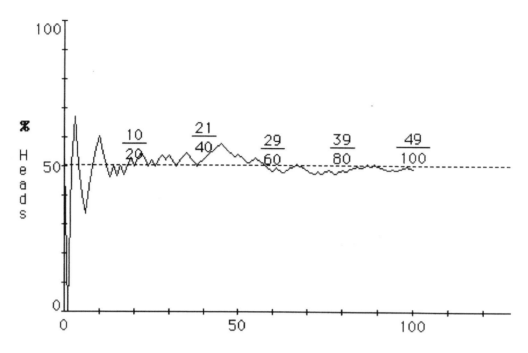

The data this graph represents are the following:

| Number of flips | Number of heads | Percent heads |
| --- | --- | --- |
| 10 | 6 | 60% |
| 20 | 10 | 50% |
| 30 | 16 | 53.3% |
| 40 | 21 | 52.5% |
| 50 | 27 | 54% |
| 60 | 29 | 48.3% |
| 70 | 34 | 48.6% |
| 80 | 39 | 48.8% |
| 90 | 45 | 50% |
| 100 | 49 | 49% |

# 1.2 • Analyzing Events

This problem is designed to help students understand the phrase *equally likely* and to recognize events that are equally likely. This concept is especially important when we later define theoretical probability.

## *Launch*

Tell the story of Kalvin's penny and his mother's suspicion that it is not a fair coin. Review his mother's example—names chosen from a hat—to illustrate the difference between events that are equally likely and those that are not equally likely.

Your students may need help understanding how the table in the problem is structured. You may want to read the first entry in the table together. The "Action" column explains the situation; the "Possible resulting events" column describes the things that can happen. Students need to decide whether the events are equally likely and explain why or why not.

Have students take a few minutes to work on the problem individually then gather in pairs or small groups to discuss their answers.

## Explore

Make sure groups understand that they should try to reach consensus about each situation. As you circulate, restrict your role to listening and asking questions. Listen to how students defend their answers, and be on the lookout for inventive ways of arguing for a particular answer.

In the follow-up, groups are challenged to describe three other situations in which the possible resulting events are equally likely and three situations in which the possible resulting events are not equally likely. Writing their own problems will deepen students' understanding of the underlying concept of equally likely. Take note of some of the clever situations that students devise.

## Summarize

Discuss the groups' answers as a class. There may be some disagreement; encourage students to explain their reasoning as they share their answers. Have groups relate some of the situations they created for the follow-up, including the situations that you noted as particularly interesting.

# Additional Answers

## Answers to Problem 1.1 Follow-Up

3. At this stage, students may not have the language or experience to answer this question thoroughly, but we want them to begin thinking about what "the chances of getting a head when you flip a coin is $\frac{1}{2}$" really means. It does not mean you will get a head one out of every two flips; it means that $\frac{1}{2}$ is a good estimate of the fraction of heads that will occur over many flips.

## Answers to Problem 1.2

D. The events are probably not equally likely, as the two teams playing are probably not exactly evenly matched. However, if sports analysts are saying the game is an even match, then winning or losing might be considered equally likely.

E. The events are roughly equally likely. Slightly more boys are born than girls.

F. The events are not equally likely. More people are right-handed than left-handed.

G. If you are truly guessing, the events are equally likely.

H. These events are probably not equally likely (unless the student's shooting average happens to be 50%). Most students will explain their answer based on their own experience with and skill at basketball.

## ACE Answers

### *Applications*

**5.** It is possible, but unlikely. Each time a coin is tossed it *can* land heads up, so 20 heads in a row is possible. However, there are many more possible combinations of 20 coin flips that are not all heads, so 20 heads is very unlikely.

---

**For the Teacher: Likelihood of 20 Heads**

Actually, the string HHHHHHHHHHHHHHHHHHHH is just as likely as any other string of 20 tosses, such as HTTHHHHTTHTHTHTHTHTT. Since there are two choices for the first position, two for the second position, and so on for all 20 positions, there are $2^{20}$ different strings that can occur. The probability of each specific string is $\frac{1}{2^{20}}$ or $\frac{1}{1,048,576}$ (roughly one in a million). Notice that there is only one way to have 20 heads in a row, but there are thousands of ways to have a mixture of heads and tails. For example, there are thousands of ways to get 10 heads and 10 tails. Hence, having some mixture of heads and tails is much more likely than having 20 heads because there are more ways to arrange them. Still, any one *specific* arrangement of 10 heads and 10 tails is just as likely (or unlikely) as a string of 20 heads.

---

# More Experiments with Chance

This investigation continues students' work with finding experimental probabilities.

In Problem 2.1, Tossing Marshmallows, students experiment with marshmallows to find a better way for Kalvin to determine his breakfast each morning. As in Problem 1.1, this problem gives students a chance to develop an understanding of probability informally, through experimentation. However, unlike the coin investigation, students do not know what results to expect when they toss marshmallows, and they gain experience with events that are not equally likely. Problem 2.2, Pondering Possible and Probable, challenges students' beliefs about the differences between *possible* and *probable*. In this problem, they analyze a two-person game of chance to determine whether it is fair. They discover that the game is not fair: although it is possible for each player to win, one player has a better chance of winning.

## Mathematical and Problem-Solving Goals

- **To gain experience finding experimental probabilities of unequally likely events**

- **To understand that chance (probability) is an estimate of behavior over the long run**

- **To understand that to make good decisions based on experimental probabilities, the probabilities must be based on a large number of trials**

- **To understand that a game of chance is fair only if each player has the same chance of winning, not just a possible chance of winning**

| Materials | | |
|---|---|---|
| **Problem** | **For students** | **For the teacher** |
| **All** | Calculators | Transparencies 2.1 and 2.2 (optional) |
| **2.1** | Large and small marshmallows (10 of each size per group; they work best if you remove them from the bag, straighten the mashed ones, and let them dry for at least a day), paper cups (optional, 1 per group) | |
| **2.2** | Pennies, (3 per group) | |

# 2.1

## Tossing Marshmallows

### Launch

- Introduce Kalvin's new plans for eating more of his favorite cereal.

- Talk about the difference between using coins and using marshmallows to generate random events.

- Discuss ways to toss marshmallows.

### Explore

- As you circulate, help pairs to conduct the experiment carefully.

- Ask questions about pairs' expectations of the variation in their results.

### Summarize

- Discuss the pairs' results and the variation in their findings.

- As a class, combine all the collected data in a table as a running total.

### Assignment Choices

ACE questions 1, 2, 4, 14–16, and unassigned choices from earlier problems

---

# More Experiments with Chance

**K**alvin loves Cocoa Blast cereal so much that he wants to find something else to flip that will give him a better chance of eating it each morning.

### 2.1 Tossing Marshmallows

Kalvin looked through the kitchen cupboard and found a bag of large marshmallows and a bag of small marshmallows. He thought that a marshmallow might be a good thing to flip, and wondered which size would be better. Since Kalvin wants to eat Cocoa Blast most of the time, he needs to find a marshmallow that lands in one position—either on its side or on one of its flat ends—most of the time. Once he decides which type of marshmallow is better, he will ask his mother if he may use the marshmallow instead of a coin for deciding his cereal each morning.

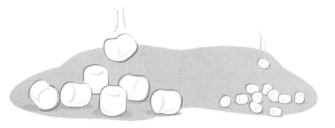

### Did you know?

**O**riginally, marshmallows were made from the root of the marsh mallow, a pink-flowered European perennial herb. Today, most marshmallows are made from corn syrup, sugar, albumen, and gelatin.

### Tips for the Linguistically Diverse Classroom

**Rebus Scenario** The Rebus Scenario technique is described in detail in *Getting to Know Connected Mathematics.* This technique involves sketching rebuses on the chalkboard that correspond to key words in the story or information you present orally. Example: some key words and phrases for which you may need to draw rebuses while discussing the material on this page: *Kalvin* (a stick figure of a boy), *kitchen cupboard* (a cupboard), *large marshmallows* (large marshmallows), *small marshmallows* (small marshmallows), *side* (a marshmallow on its side), *flat end* (a marshmallow on its end), *coin* (a coin).

## Problem 2.1

Experiment with large and small marshmallows to help you answer these questions:

**A.** Which size marshmallow should Kalvin use to determine which cereal he will eat? Explain your answer.

**B.** Which of the marshmallow's landing positions—end or side—should Kalvin use to represent Cocoa Blast? Explain your answer.

To conduct your experiment, toss each size of marshmallow 50 times. Keep track of your data carefully. Here is an example of how you might want to organize your data:

|  | Lands on an end | Lands on side |
|---|---|---|
| Large marshmallow | ⫫⫫ ꞁ | ꞁꞁꞁꞁ |
| Small marshmallow |  |  |

Use the results of your experiment to help you answer questions A and B.

### ▓ Problem 2.1 Follow-Up

Work with your teacher to combine results from all the groups.

**1. a.** For what fraction of your 50 tosses did the large marshmallow land on one of its ends? On its side?

 **b.** For what fraction of the class's tosses did the large marshmallow land on one of its ends? On its side?

 **c.** If you toss a large marshmallow once each day for a year, how many times would you expect it to land on its side?

**2. a.** For what fraction of your 50 tosses did the small marshmallow land on one of its ends? On its side?

 **b.** For what fraction of the class's tosses did the small marshmallow land on one of its ends? On its side?

 **c.** If you toss a small marshmallow once each day for a year, how many times would you expect it to land on its side?

**3.** Suppose Kalvin uses the marshmallow you chose—large or small—to decide his cereal each morning. He tosses the marshmallow twice, and it lands on an end once and on its side once. He says, "This marshmallow isn't any better than the penny—it lands on an end 50% of the time!" How would you convince Kalvin that the marshmallow is better for him to use than a penny?

## Answers to Problem 2.1

Answers will vary. Students should justify their answers using the results of their experiment.

## Answers to Problem 2.1 Follow-Up

1. Answers will vary.

2. Answers will vary.

3. Possible answer: You would need to tell Kalvin that two trials are not enough to give a good estimate of the chances that the marshmallow will land on an end or its side. Kalvin needs to toss the marshmallow lots of times to make a good estimate.

# Pondering Possible and Probable

## At a Glance

### Grouping:
### Pairs

### Launch

- Play a couple of rounds of the coin-tossing game with the class.

- Discuss the difference between games of chance and games of skill.

### Explore

- As you circulate, remind students that they must be able to explain their answers.

- Challenge students who finish quickly to revise the game to make it fair.

### Summarize

- As a class, combine results and determine the relative frequencies of getting three of a kind and two of a kind.

- Have students list all possible outcomes of a toss of three coins. (*optional*)

### 2.2 Pondering Possible and Probable

Jon and Tat Ming are playing a coin-tossing game. To play the game, they take turns tossing three coins. If all three of the coins match, Jon scores a point. If only two of the coins match, Tat Ming scores a point. The first player to get 5 points wins. Both players have won the game several times, but Tat Ming seems to be winning more often. Jon says that he thinks the game is unfair. Tat Ming claims that the game is fair because both of them have a chance to win.

What do you think? Is the game fair as long as it is possible for each player to win?

### Problem 2.2

Conduct an experiment to help you answer these questions:

**A.** Is it possible for Jon to win the game? Is it possible for Tat Ming to win the game? Explain your reasoning.

**B.** Who is more likely to win? Why?

**C.** Is this a fair game of chance? Explain.

To conduct your experiment, toss three coins 30 times. Keep track of the number of times three coins match and the number of times only two coins match. Be sure to organize your data and give reasons for your conclusions.

### ▓ Problem 2.2 Follow-Up

**1.** If you tossed the coins 30 more times, how many times would you expect the three coins to match?

**2.** Toss the coins 30 more times. Compare this set of results to your first set of results. Did the three coins match about the same number of times in each experiment?

## Assignment Choices

ACE questions 3, 5–13, 17, and unassigned choices from earlier problems

## Answers to Problem 2.2

A. Since it is possible for only two of the three coins or for all three coins to match, it is possible for either player to win.

B. Tat Ming is more likely to win, because the chances of two coins matching are greater than the chances of three coins matching. (The actual probability that Tat Ming scores is $\frac{3}{4}$, and the probability that Jon scores is $\frac{1}{4}$.)

C. No, this is not a fair game of chance. Tat Ming has more chances to score, since he must match only two coins.

## Answers to Problem 2.2 Follow-Up

See page 21c.

# ACE

**Applications • Connections • Extensions**

As you work on these ACE questions, use your calculator whenever you need it.

## Applications

**1.** When you toss a marshmallow, are the chances that it will land on an end the same as the chances that it will land on its side? That is, are the two events equally likely? Explain your reasoning.

**2.** If Kalvin uses the size marshmallow that you chose in Problem 2.1, how many times a month would you expect him to eat Cocoa Blast? How many times a year? Explain your reasoning.

**3.** Dawn tossed a pawn from her chess set 5 times. It landed on its base 4 times and on its side only once. Dawn decided that the pawn lands on its base more often than on its side.

Andre tossed the same pawn 100 times. It landed on its base 28 times and on its side 72 times. Andre decided the pawn lands on its side more often than its base.

Based on Andre and Dawn's data, if you toss the pawn one more time, do you think it would be more likely to land on its base or its side? Why?

## Connections

**4.** Meteorologists make many claims about the chances of rain, sun, and snow occurring. Waldo, the meteorologist from WARM radio, claims he is the best weather predictor in Sunspot, South Carolina. On the day before Sunspot High's graduation ceremony, Waldo said: "There is only a 10% chance of rain tomorrow!"

**Investigation 2: More Experiments with Chance**  **17**

## Answers

### Applications

**1.** no; Explanations will vary depending on the experimental probabilities students found.

**2.** Answers will vary depending on the experimental probabilities students found.

**3.** On its side, because it is better to base a prediction on 100 tosses than on 5 tosses. It would give us even more information if we combined the data; the results would be that the pawn landed on its base 32 out of 105 tosses, which means it is more likely to land on its side.

**Investigation 2**  **17**

## Connections

**4a.** Answers will vary. Some may say this means that in weather conditions like these, it rains one out of every ten days. Others may say that if the conditions are covering a large area, it will rain on $\frac{1}{10}$ of the area. You might extend this question and ask for volunteers to call a local television or radio station to ask a weather reporter's opinion.

**4b.** Answers will vary.

**4c.** no; A 10% chance of rain does not mean that it will not rain, just that it is not very likely to rain.

**5–11.** Answers will vary. Students' answers should be fractions between and including 0 and 1 (or percents between and including 0 and 100), and their reasoning should justify the answer.

**a.** Ask at least two adults what they think Waldo's statement means, and write down their explanations.

**b.** Explain what you think Waldo's statement means.

**c.** If it rains on the graduation ceremony, was Waldo wrong? Why or why not?

You can use a fraction or a percent to indicate the chances that a particular event will occur. The larger the fraction or percent, the greater the chances that the event will happen. If an event is impossible, the chances that it will occur are 0, or 0%. If an event is sure to happen, the chances that it will occur are 1, or 100%.

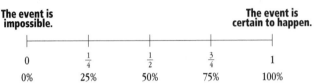

In 5–12, assign a number from 0 to 1 to indicate the chances that the event will occur, and explain your reasoning. For example, if the event is, "You will watch television tonight," your answer might be this:

*I watch some television every night unless I have too much homework. So far today I do not have much homework. Therefore, I am about 95% sure that I will watch television tonight.*

**5.** You will be absent from school at least one day during this school year.

**6.** You will have pizza for lunch one day this week.

**7.** It will snow on July 4 this year in Mexico.

**8.** You will get all the problems on your next math test correct.

**9.** The next baby born in your local hospital will be a girl.

**10.** The sun will set tonight.

**11.** You will win a coin-tossing game by tossing four coins, all of which must land heads.

**12.** You will toss a coin and get 100 tails in a row.

**13.** Make up two of your own events, and then estimate the chances that each event will happen.

In 14–16, use the chart below, which shows the percent of people who have been fired from a job for various reasons.

### Reasons People Are Fired

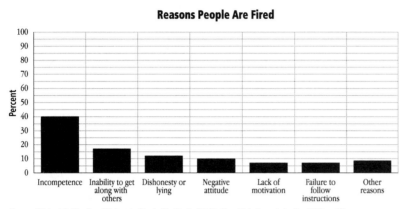

Source: Michael D. Shook and Robert L. Shook, *The Book of Odds* (New York: Penguin books, 1991), p. 53.

**14.** If this chart represents 5000 people, about how many of these people were fired because they could not get along with others? Explain your reasoning.

**15.** What fraction of the people represented in the chart were fired for reasons other than incompetence? Explain more than one way that you could find the answer to this question.

**16.** If the chart represents 5000 people, about how many were fired for dishonesty or lying? Explain.

**12.** Answers will vary. Students' answers should be fractions between and including 0 and 1 (or percents between and including 0 and 100), close to 0, and their reasoning should justify the answer.

**13.** Answers will vary.

**14.** about 850 people; About 17% of the people were fired for inability to get along with others, and 5000 × 0.17 = 850 people.

**15.** about 60%; Add the percents for all the reasons except incompetence or subtract 40% from 100%.

**16.** about 600 people; About 12% of the 5000 people were fired for lying or dishonesty, which is about 5000 × 0.12 = 600 people. (**Teaching Tip:** Students may say that the data in questions 14–16 is oversimplified; many people probably get fired for more than one reason. You might use this as an opportunity to discuss how data is sometimes summarized and simplified to communicate it to the general population.)

## Extensions

**17a.** Since the cup landed upright 5 times out of 50, Yolanda can expect to win about 1 out of 10 times.

**17b.** less; Yolanda would have to spend $10 to play 10 times. She should expect to win once, giving her $5, so she will have spent $5 more than she won. Of course, this is only a good guess about what to expect. She may actually lose more money or win money. She can expect to lose 9 out of 10 times!

# Extensions

**17.** While Yolanda was at a carnival, she watched a game in which a paper cup was tossed. If the cup landed upright, the player won $5. It cost $1 to play the game. Yolanda watched the cup being tossed 50 times. The cup landed on its side 32 times, upside down 13 times, and upright 5 times.

**a.** If Yolanda plays the game 10 times, about how many times can she expect to win? How many times can she expect to lose?

**b.** Would you expect Yolanda to have more or less money at the end of 10 games than she had before? Why?

# Mathematical Reflections

In this investigation, you conducted an experiment that involved tossing marshmallows. You also experimented with a coin-tossing game to determine whether it was fair. These questions will help you summarize what you have learned:

1. When you toss a large marshmallow, is it equally likely to land on an end as its side? What evidence can you use to help you answer this question?

2. How would you use the results of your work in Problem 2.1 to predict how many times a small marshmallow would land on its side if you tossed it 1000 times?

3. What does it mean for a two-person game of chance to be fair?

4. In a–f, give an example of an event that would have about the given chances of occurring.

   **a.** 0%          **b.** 10%

   **c.** 25%         **d.** 50%

   **e.** 75%         **f.** 100%

Think about your answers to these questions, discuss your ideas with other students and your teacher, and then write a summary of your findings in your journal.

## Tips for the Linguistically Diverse Classroom

**Diagram Code** The Diagram Code technique is described in detail in *Getting to Know Connected Mathematics*. Students use a minimal number of words and drawings, diagrams, or symbols to respond to questions that require writing. Example: Question 3—A student might answer this question by drawing two stick figures each labeled with the words *50% chance to win*.

## Possible Answers

1. no; While students' data may vary, a large marshmallow seems to land on an end about $\frac{1}{4}$ of the time. Students should present the results of their experiments to support their thinking.

2. I would take the data on the number of times a small marshmallow landed on its side and the number of times the marshmallow was tossed and write that as a fraction. Then I would find an equivalent fraction for that amount with a denominator of 1000. The numerator of the new fraction would tell me the number of times the marshmallow might land on its side if I tossed it 1000 times.

3. It means that each person has the same chance of winning.

**4a.** 0%: It will be 110° in Michigan on the first of January.

**4b.** 10%: There will be a great parking place at the game.

**4c.** 25%: I will eat a hamburger for lunch.

**4d.** 50%: A pog will land heads up when I flip it.

**4e.** 75%: It will snow during a week of winter in New York.

**4f.** 100%: I will wear shoes outdoors in the winter.

# TEACHING THE INVESTIGATION

## 2.1 • Tossing Marshmallows

This is students' first exposure to a situation in which experimentation is necessary for getting a sense of behavior; a theoretical analysis of the behavior of a marshmallow being tossed is not available. Students will toss marshmallows and determine this fraction:

$$P(end) = \frac{\text{number of times a marshmallow lands on an end}}{\text{total number of tosses}}$$

## Launch

Tell the story of Kalvin's plans for eating more Cocoablast. Before students begin the experiment, ask them to predict which marshmallow—large or small—and which landing position—end or side—would be best for Kalvin to use.

Talk with your students about the differences between using coins and marshmallows to generate random events:

> Will marshmallows behave like pennies and land on an end or a side about the same number of times? Why or why not?

At this stage, you want students to begin to suspect that marshmallows may not behave as coins behave.

Also discuss procedures for tossing the marshmallows. Students can generate 50 tosses quickly by putting 10 marshmallows into a cup, shaking the cup, and tossing the marshmallows. Be sure they understand the suggested method for keeping track of their results. You want students, over time, to decide on record-keeping schemes for themselves, but they do need a few models.

Have students work in pairs or small groups on the problem.

## Explore

As you visit groups while they work, help them to be careful about gathering their data and organizing their results. Ask whether they think their results and other pairs' results will be the same. Through your questions, try to encourage them to realize that there will be a great deal of variation among individual sets of 50 tosses, but less variation in the class's combined results.

## Summarize

After pairs have each tossed the marshmallows 50 times, discuss their findings.

> Did you all arrive at the same conclusion about which marshmallow and which landing position Kalvin should use? Why or why not?

Combine the data from all the pairs, and find the fraction (or percent) of times each type of marshmallow landed on its side or an end. As in Problem 1.1, you can add the data for each group one at a time, refiguring the fractions (or percents) with each addition so students can see when the relative frequency of landing on an end begins to level off.

Discuss the follow-up as a class. The questions will help students to summarize the results of their marshmallow-tossing experiment.

# 2.2 • Pondering Possible and Probable

Many students believe that *possible* and *probable* mean the same thing and that a game of chance is fair if each player has a *chance* to win, even if it is not *equally likely* that each player will win. This problem directly challenges these beliefs.

## Launch

A good launching strategy is to play the coin-tossing game with the class so students understand how to score and take turns. This is a fairly simple game; a couple of rounds will probably be sufficient.

Initiate a discussion about what it means for a game to be fair:

> What do you think it means to say that a game is a fair game?

Here are some responses students have given.

- Josh said, "No one cheats!"
- Diane said, "Everyone has a chance to win."
- Hani said, "The players are equally good."

Make sure students understand that you are referring to games of chance (like bingo) rather than games of skill (like tennis). You might want to bring up games at fairs and carnivals.

> Who has better chances of winning—the player or the house?

The coin-tossing game is a two-person game, so students need to think in terms of two players. In fair games of chance, each player has an equal chance, or probability, of winning.

When students understand that they are to examine Jon and Tat Ming's game for fairness, let them play the game in pairs and gather data to help answer the questions.

## Explore

As you listen to students discuss the game, remind them that they must be prepared to explain why they think the game is fair or unfair. Give an extra challenge to students who immediately understand that the chances of three coins matching are less than the chances of two coins matching:

> Can you think of a way to make the game fair?

## Summarize

In the summary of the problem, you again have an opportunity to let students discover the variability in the results of all the games that were played. The follow-up examines this variability by having each group repeat their experiment and look at their two sets of data. This variability in the short run, and predictability over many trials is the heart of understanding chance phenomena. As a class, have students examine their records and combine data to figure out how many times they got three of a kind and two of a kind. From this data, you and the class can determine relative frequencies of getting all heads, all tails, or a matching pair. The relative frequencies will demonstrate that the game is unfair.

Students do not analyze situations by listing all the possible outcomes until Investigation 4, but some may be ready to list all the possible outcomes from the tossing of three coins:

TTT   TTH   THT   HTT   THH   HTH   HHT   HHH

Each of the eight possibilities has the same chance of occurring—the individual outcomes are equally likely. However, in this game we are interested in three of a kind or a pair. The probabilities are as follows:

$$P(\text{three heads or three tails}) = 2(\tfrac{1}{8}) = \tfrac{2}{8} = \tfrac{1}{4}$$

$$P(\text{two heads or two tails}) = 6(\tfrac{1}{8}) = \tfrac{6}{8} = \tfrac{3}{4}$$

This means that one player has much better chances of scoring and hence winning.

---

### For the Teacher: Outcomes and Events

An *outcome* is one of the possible results of an action. For example, the eight possible outcomes of tossing three coins are TTT, TTH, THT, HTT, THH, HTH, HHT, and HHH. An *event* is a subset of the set of possible outcomes. In the example above, three matching coins is an event made up of the outcomes TTT and HHH. If all the possible outcomes of an action are equally likely, then the theoretical probability of an event occurring is $\frac{\text{the number of outcomes in the event}}{\text{the total number of outcomes}}$. So, the theoretical probability the three coins match is $\tfrac{2}{8}$, or $\tfrac{1}{4}$. It is not neccesary for students to distinguish between an event and an outcome to solve the problems in this unit.

---

# Additional Answers

## Answers to Problem 2.2 Follow-Up

1. Most students will predict the same frequency they got in the first experiment because they have no other information to use.

2. Answers will vary. However, most groups will get a different distribution of results on the second set of 30 tosses. (Listing the results for each group will help students understand the variablity in small samples. Then, combine the data so the number of trials is large. Ask the class how confident they are about their own samples compared to the combined class sample.)

# Using Spinners to Predict Chances

This is the last investigation in which probabilities are dealt with informally and experimentally. In the next investigation, probability is formally defined, and students will begin working with theoretical probabilities.

In this investigation, Kalvin—trying to make a deal with his father about a new bedtime for the summer—makes a spinner with spaces representing possible bedtimes. Using spinners allows students to connect probability to the area of a circle. This unit follows the *Covering and Surrounding* unit, in which students found areas and perimeters of circles. However, making pie charts (circle graphs) was not a part of the data unit, *Data About Us,* so you may need to help students connect the measure of a central angle to the part of the total area a section of a circle occupies.

In Problem 3.1, Bargaining for a Better Bedtime, students experiment with Kalvin's spinner to see which bedtime will occur most often. The number of trials for the experiment is not specified; students are to decide for themselves when they have collected enough data to make a good prediction.

## Mathematical and Problem-Solving Goals

- **To develop strategies for finding experimental probabilities with a new simulation tool: spinners**

- **To understand that to make good decisions based on experimental probabilities, the probabilities must be based on a large number of trials**

| Materials | | |
|---|---|---|
| **Problem** | **For students** | **For the teacher** |
| **All** | Calculators | |
| **3.1** | Labsheet 3.1 (1 per group); bobby pins or paper clips (for making spinners, 1 per group) | Transparency 3.1 (optional), Transparency of Labsheet 3.1 (optional) |
| **ACE** | Labsheet 3.ACE | |

# Bargaining for a Better Bedtime

*Grouping:*
*Pairs or Small Groups*

## Launch

- Ask students to predict which bedtime they think will occur most often on Kalvin's spinner.

- Be sure students understand that *they* must decide when they have collected enough data.

## Explore

- As you circulate, watch for spinning techniques that might bias the data.

- Help students to determine whether they have collected enough data.

- Have students work on the follow-up.

## Summarize

- Discuss findings and, as a class, combine all the data in a table.

- Help students to relate the experimental and theoretical probabilities.

## Assignment Choices

ACE questions 1–12 (1 requires a paper clip or bobby pin) and unassigned choices from earlier problems

---

# Using Spinners to Predict Chances

**S**chool is out for the summer! Kalvin thinks he should be allowed to stay up until midnight every night since he doesn't have to get up for school in the morning. His father disagrees; he thinks Kalvin will have more energy for all the things he plans to do in the summer if he goes to bed earlier.

## 3.1 Bargaining for a Better Bedtime

Kalvin decided to make a spinner that he hopes his father will let him use to determine his bedtime each night. To encourage his father to go for his idea, Kalvin put three 10:00 and three 11:00 spaces on the spinner. However, he used the biggest space for 12:00, and he hopes the spinner will land on that space most often. Kalvin's spinner is shown on the next page.

### Problem 3.1

Conduct an experiment to help you answer these questions.

**A.** Kalvin prefers to go to bed at midnight, so he wants his spinner to land on 12:00 more often than anywhere else. Is it likely that this spinner will allow him to achieve this goal? Explain.

**B.** Suppose Kalvin's father lets him use this spinner to determine his bedtime. What are Kalvin's chances of going to bed at 12:00? Explain how you determined your answer.

To conduct your experiment, use Labsheet 3.1 and a bobby pin or paper clip to make a spinner like Kalvin's. Spin the spinner, and keep track of the data you collect. Continue spinning the spinner and recording data until you are confident about your answers to the questions above.

## Assessment

It is appropriate to use the quiz and Check-Up 1 after this problem. The quiz involves collecting data; look over the preparation notes carefully.

## Answers to Problem 3.1

A. no; His spinner will land on 10:00 most often because the 10:00 spaces make up the largest part of the spinner.

B. His chances of going to bed at 12:00 are $\frac{1}{3}$ or about 33%.

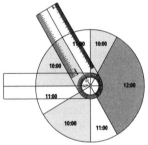

### ▦ Problem 3.1 Follow-Up

**1.** After how many spins did you decide to stop spinning? Why? If you continued to spin the spinner, do you think your answers to Problem 3.1 would change? Why or why not?

**2. a.** How many times did you spin the spinner? How many times did the spinner land on 10:00? On 11:00? On 12:00?

   **b.** Based on your data, what fraction of the time will Kalvin go to bed at 10:00? At 11:00? At 12:00?

   **c.** Summer vacation is 90 days long. If Kalvin uses this spinner every night, how many nights do you think he will go to bed at 10:00? At 11:00? At 12:00? Explain your reasoning.

**3.** In a–c, use your angle ruler or other ways of reasoning to analyze Kalvin's spinner. You can set your angle ruler on the spinner to measure the angle of each section.

   **a.** What fraction of the area of the spinner is made up of 10:00 spaces? Of 11:00 spaces? Of 12:00 spaces?

   **b.** How do the fractions from part a compare with the fractions you found in part b of question 2?

   **c.** How do the fractions from part a compare with the fractions from the data your entire class collected for Problem 3.1?

## Answers to Problem 3.1 Follow-Up

1. Answers will vary. Students should have watched for patterns in their data and stopped when the percents corresponding to each bedtime leveled off, and new data had little effect on the percents.

2. a. Answers will vary.

   b. Answers will vary, but if students did enough trials they should report that Kalvin will go to bed at 10:00 about $\frac{5}{12}$ of the time, at 11:00 about $\frac{1}{4}$ of the time, and at 12:00 about $\frac{1}{3}$ of the time.

   c. See page 28b.

3. See page 28b.

## Answers

### Applications

1. See pages 28b and 28c.

As you work on these ACE questions, use your calculator whenever you need it.

# Applications

1. In a–g, use the spinner on Labsheet 3.ACE.

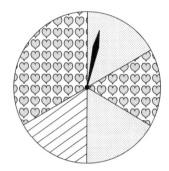

   a. Use a paper clip or bobby pin to spin the spinner 30 times. What fraction of your spins landed on a space with hearts? With dots? With stripes?

   b. Use your angle ruler or another method to analyze the spinner. What fraction of the spinner is covered with hearts? With dots? With stripes? Explain how you found each fraction.

   c. Compare your answers to parts a and b. Would you expect these answers to be the same? Why or why not?

   d. If you were to spin the spinner 300 times instead of 30 times, do you think your answers would become closer to or further from the fractions you found in part b? Explain your reasoning.

   e. When you spin the spinner, are the three possible outcomes—landing on a space with hearts, landing on a space with dots, and landing on a space with stripes—equally likely? Explain.

   f. Suppose you use the spinner to play a game with a friend. Your friend scores a point every time the spinner lands on a space with hearts. What spaces should you score on to make the game fair? Explain your reasoning.

   g. Suppose you use this spinner to play a three-person game. Player A scores if the spinner lands on stripes. Player B scores if the spinner lands on hearts. Player C scores if the spinner lands on dots. How could you allocate points so the game would be fair?

**2.** Mollie is designing a game for a class project. She made the three spinners shown here and experimented with them to see which one she liked best for her game. She spun each spinner 20 times and wrote down her results, but she forgot to record which spinner gave which set of data. Which spinner most likely gave each data set? Explain your answer.

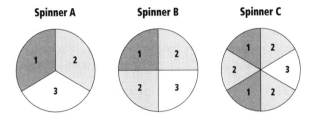

**Spinner A**   **Spinner B**   **Spinner C**

First data set
1 2 3 2 1 1 2 1 2 2 2 3 2 1 2 2 2 3 2 2

Second data set
2 3 1 1 3 3 3 1 1 2 3 2 2 2 1 1 1 3 3 3

Third data set
1 2 3 3 1 2 2 2 3 2 1 2 2 2 3 2 2 3 2 1

**3.** Three people play a game on each of the spinners in question 2. Player 1 scores a point if the spinner lands on an area marked 1, player 2 scores a point if the spinner lands on an area marked 2, and player 3 scores a point if the spinner lands on an area marked 3.

**a.** On which spinner or spinners would the game be a fair game of chance? Why?

**b.** Choose a spinner that you think would not make a fair game of chance with these rules. Then, change the scoring rules to make the game fair by assigning different points for landing on the different numbers. Explain why your point system works.

**2.** Answers will vary. The answer that brings the experimental probabilities as close as possible to the theoretical probabilities is this one: the first data set (5 ones, 12 twos, 3 threes) is from spinner C; the second data set (7 ones, 5 twos, 8 threes) is from spinner A; and the third data set (4 ones, 11 twos, 5 threes) is from spinner B. Students might argue that 20 trials are not enough to be certain which spinner generated which data set, and this is certainly true.

**3a.** spinner A; Each player has the same amount of area in which to score.

**3b.** See page 28c.

**4.** Answers will vary.

**Connections**

**5.** Although more people were killed in cars according to the data, motorcycles are not necessarily safer. We need information on how many people drive cars and how many drive motorcycles, and the number of hours they spend on the road.

**6.** about 20% (half of 40%)

**7.** More motorcycle-related deaths occur on weekends according to the data, but this does not mean that any individual motorcycle rider is in more danger of being killed on the weekend than during the week. There could be more deaths on weekends because more people drive motorcycles on the weekend.

**8.** More males are victims of fatal crashes according to the data, but they aren't necessarily worse drivers than females. To answer this question, we would need to know the number of hours males spend driving versus the number of hours females spend driving. Furthermore, we would need to know what proportion of fatal crashes males are responsible for, because the given information relates only to victims of fatal crashes, not drivers who are in fatal crashes.

**4. a.** Create a spinner and a set of rules for a two-person game that would be a fair game.

   **b.** Create a spinner and a set of rules for a two-person game that would not be fair. Explain how you could change the rules to make the game fair.

# Connections

In 5–9, use the data below to answer the question. If there is not enough information to answer a question, explain what additional information you would need.

- In 1988, 47,093 people were killed in car crashes and 3486 people were killed in motorcycle crashes in the United States.
- In the U.S., 40% of all deaths of people between the ages of 15 and 19 result from motor-vehicle crashes. Alcohol is involved in about half of these crashes.
- Males outnumber females as fatal-crash victims by an average of 2 to 1.
- 55% of motorcycle deaths occurred on weekends.
- In 1988, the car with the lowest death rate was the Volvo 740/760 four-door, while the car with the highest death rate was the Chevrolet Corvette.

Source: Michael D. Shook and Robert L. Shook, *The Book of Odds* (New York: Penguin Books, 1991), p. 90.

**5.** Which is safer to drive, a car or a motorcycle?

**6.** What percent of all deaths of 15-year-olds to 19-year-olds result from alcohol-related motor-vehicle crashes?

**7.** Is a particular motorcycle rider more likely to be in a fatal crash during the week or during the weekend?

**8.** Are males worse drivers than females?

**9.** Your family is trying to decide which used car to buy. Are you less likely to have an accident if you buy a Volvo 740 or Volvo 760 than if you buy a Chevrolet Corvette?

# Extensions

**10.** Design a spinner with five spaces so that the chances of landing in each space are equally likely. Give the number of degrees in the central angle of each space.

**11.** Design a spinner with five spaces so that the chances of landing in each space are not equally likely. Give the number of degrees in the central angle of each space.

**12.** Design a spinner with five spaces so that the chances of landing in one space are twice the chances of landing in each of the other four spaces. Give the number of degrees in the central angle of each space.

**9.** The question asks about having an accident, but there is no data about this, only about death rates. **(Teaching Tip:** Students may want to discuss the possibility of dying in either car. According to the data, more deaths occurred in a Chevrolet Corvette than in a Volvo 740 or a Volvo 760, but this does not mean that a potential car buyer is more likely to be killed in one car than the other. The people who drive these particular cars could have made the difference, rather than the cars themselves.)

### Extensions

**10.**

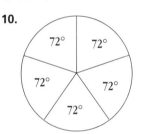

**11.** Possible answer:

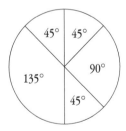

**12.**

## Possible Answers

**1.** The fraction of times the spinner landed on region A is $\frac{306}{400}$, which is about 76%, or $\frac{3}{4}$, of the time. The spinner could be divided so that region A makes up about $\frac{3}{4}$ of the total area and region B makes up about $\frac{1}{4}$ of the total area. Since the number of trials is large, I can be fairly confident that the spinner looks like this.

**2.** Since $\frac{13}{20} = 65\%$, we can guess that region A makes up 65% of the area and region B makes up 35% of the area. Since there are only 20 trials, I cannot be very confident about my guess. This spinner could be the same spinner in question 1, since 13 A's and 7 B's is not very different from the 15 A's and 5 B's that would be expected on that spinner.

**3.** I would divide the spinner into four equal sections and mark each section in a different way. Each section would have a central angle of 90°.

**4.** It is possible, but very unlikely!

---

# Mathematical Reflections

**I**n this investigation, you experimented with spinners. When you spin a spinner, you cannot know in advance which section it will land on, but you can conduct an experiment to gather data that will help you to predict what will happen over many trials. These questions will help you summarize what you have learned:

**1** Suppose that out of 400 spins, a spinner lands 306 times on region A and 94 times on region B. What can you say about the spinner? What might the spinner look like? How confident are you in your answer? Explain.

**2** Suppose that out of 20 spins, a spinner lands 13 times on region A and 7 times on region B. What can you say about the spinner? What might the spinner look like? How confident are you in your answer? Explain.

**3** Describe how you could construct a spinner with four equally likely outcomes.

**4** Look back at Kalvin's bedtime spinner for Problem 3.1. Is it possible that the spinner will land on 12:00 each night for a month? Is it likely?

Think about your answers to these questions, discuss your ideas with other students and your teacher, and then write a summary of your findings in your journal.

---

## Tips for the Linguistically Diverse Classroom

**Diagram Code** The Diagram Code technique is described in detail in *Getting to Know Connected Mathematics*. Students use a minimal number of words and drawings, diagrams, or symbols to respond to questions that require writing. Example: Question 1—A student might answer this question by drawing a spinner in which section A makes up about $\frac{3}{4}$ of the total area, and section B makes up about $\frac{1}{4}$ of the total area. Section A might be labeled $\frac{306}{400}$ (76%), and a label under the spinner might read confident because 400 spins.

# TEACHING THE INVESTIGATION

## 3.1 • Bargaining for a Better Bedtime

In this problem, students find experimental probabilities associated with a spinner. Students are not told how many times to spin the spinner. They must decide for themselves when they have enough data to make a good prediction.

### Launch

Discuss Kalvin's idea about determining his bedtime with a spinner.

> Predict which bedtime you think Kalvin is most likely to spin using the spinner. Explain your prediction.

Some students may choose 12:00 because it occupies the largest section of the circle; some may say 10:00 or 11:00 because they each occupy three sections; and some may be able to analyze the chances based on the fraction of the total area each bedtime represents. (We will return to the idea of comparing the areas in follow-up question 3.)

Demonstrate a couple of spins, using a transparency of Labsheet 3.1 if possible. Place the point of a sharpened pencil or a pen through the circular end of a bobby pin or paper clip and on the center of the spinner. Flick the bobby pin with your finger. Record your data, demonstrating how to keep a tally for each spin. After spinning two or three times, ask whether you have a large enough sample. Students should realize that a couple of spins does not generate enough data to predict the behavior of the spinner over the long run.

Distribute Labsheet 3.1 to each pair or group of students. Be sure students understand that *they* must decide when they feel certain enough of their results to stop collecting data.

### Explore

As you circulate, ask questions that encourage students to pay attention to the spinning techniques they are using. Are they introducing a tendency for the spinner to land in the same area each time? Such bias will affect the data so that a good prediction of how the spinner will behave under more random spinning conditions cannot be made.

If the chances of two of the bedtimes seem very close from the data a group has generated so far, encourage the group to keep spinning until they are fairly certain about which time is more likely to occur. As groups finish, have them move on to follow-up questions 1 and 2.

Question 3 is especially important and may be done as a whole class during the summary. Students may find the answers to part a in several ways. Some will measure the central angle for each section of the spinner, add up the measures for each bedtime, and divide each total by 360°. Some may measure the angles by cutting out and rearranging the sections so all of the 10:00 sections are together and all of the 11:00 sections are together. Some will be able to determine visually the portion of the area each section represents. Others may realize that if they were to divide the spinner into 12 equal sections, the 10:00 spaces would occupy 5 sections, the 11:00 spaces would occupy 3 sections, and the 12:00 space would occupy 4 sections.

## Summarize

Discuss the data that groups collected and their answers to the questions. Their answers may vary because the numbers of trials some groups conducted may not have been large enough to pick up the differences among the three fractions.

As in previous investigations, combine the data for all the groups, recalculating the fractions or percents after each groups' data is added. Students should conclude that the spinner is not a good deal for Kalvin: the chances of a 10:00 bedtime are $\frac{5}{12}$ (42%), the chances of an 11:00 bedtime are $\frac{3}{12}$ (25%), and the chances of a 12:00 bedtime are $\frac{4}{12}$ (33%).

To summarize this activity, discuss the follow-up questions. Pay particular attention to question 3, which connects the experimental probabilities to the areas of the spinner sections. The fractions calculated in part a are actually the theoretical probabilities. However, the term *theoretical probability* is not formally introduced until Investigation 4.

One effective way to relate this problem to Problem 1.1 is to make a graph of the total number of spins versus the percent of 12:00 spins. For example, suppose one group's spinner landed on 12:00 on 5 out of 20 spins, or 25% of the time. Plot (20, 25%) as the first point on the graph. For the next point, use the combined data from the first group and the second group. If the second group got 12:00 in 10 out of 25 spins, the total for the first two groups would be 15 out of 45 spins, and you would plot (45, 33%) on the graph. Continue plotting points until you have included the results for every group. The experimental probability should close in on the theoretical probability as the number of trials increases.

# Additional Answers

## Answers to Problem 3.1 Follow-Up

2. c. Kalvin would go to bed at 10:00 about 37 or 38 times (since $\frac{5}{12} \times 90 = 37.5$), at 11:00 about 22 or 23 times (since $\frac{1}{4} \times 90 = 22.5$), and at 12:00 about 30 times (since $\frac{1}{3} \times 90 = 30$).

3. a. The 10:00 spaces make up $\frac{5}{12}$ of the spinner's area (or 150° of the 360°), the 11:00 spaces make up $\frac{1}{4}$ of the area (90° of the 360°), and the 12:00 space makes up $\frac{1}{3}$ of the area (120° of the 360°).

   b. Answers will vary, but if students did enough trials, the fractions should be close.

   c. Answers will vary, but the fractions should be close.

## ACE Answers

### Applications

**1a.** about $\frac{1}{2}$ for hearts, $\frac{1}{3}$ for dots, and $\frac{1}{6}$ for stripes

**1b.** Possible answer: I divided the large heart section in half, and then I could see that the spinner has six equal sections. The hearts occupy $\frac{3}{6}$, the dots $\frac{2}{6}$, and the stripes $\frac{1}{6}$.

**1c.** Possible answer: These answers are not likely to be exactly the same, but if we do many trials they should be close.

**1d.** Possible answer: My answers should be closer to the actual fractions because I would be using more data to determine them.

**1e.** no; The fractions of the total area the different patterns make up are not the same. For example, there is a greater chance of landing on a space with hearts than a space with dots, because the area covered with hearts ($\frac{1}{2}$ of the total area) is greater than the area covered with dots ($\frac{1}{3}$ of the total area).

**1f.** Possible answers: I could score a point on both dots and stripes to make the game fair. This would give half the area to each of us. Or, I could score three points for landing on stripes, and neither of us could score when the spinner lands on dots.

**1g.** Possible answer: In 36 spins, player A would expect to score about 6 times, player B would expect to score about 18 times, and player C would expect to score about 12 times. To make the points each player would accumulate the same, we can let player A score 3 points each time the spinner lands on stripes, player B score 1 point each time the spinner lands on hearts, and player C score $1\frac{1}{2}$ points each time the spinner lands on dots; this would give an expected 18 points for each player for 36 spins. Or, you could let player A score 6 points, player B score 2 points, and player C score 3 points; then each would expect 36 points for 36 spins.

---

### For the Teacher: Preparing for ACE Question 1

You may want to discuss question 1 in class. You want students to make the connection between their data and their measurements. Emphasize that since half of the spinner is covered with hearts, we expect—over the long run—to get hearts for about half of all spins. The theoretical probabilities should be fairly close to the experimental probabilities—*if the experimental probabilities are based on a large number of trials.*

Part g is harder than part f, because students have to see that the expectation must be the same for all players over some number of spins.

---

**3b.** Possible answers: On spinner B, the 1 section makes up $\frac{1}{4}$ of the area, the 2 sections make up $\frac{2}{4}$ of the area, and the 3 section makes up $\frac{1}{4}$ of the area. In four spins, player 1 could expect to score once, player 2 could expect to score twice, and player 3 could expect to score once. To make the game fair, you could give 2 points to player 1 if the spinner lands on 1, 1 point to player 2 if the spinner lands on 2, and 2 points to player 3 if the spinner lands on 3. In 8 spins, player 1 could expect to score twice for a total of $2 \times 2 = 4$ points, player 2 could expect to score four times for a total of $4 \times 1 = 4$ points, and player 3 could expect to score twice for a total of $2 \times 2 = 4$ points.

On spinner C, the 1 sections make up $\frac{2}{6}$ of the area, the 2 sections make up $\frac{3}{6}$ of the area, and the 3 section makes up $\frac{1}{6}$ of the area. In 6 spins, player 1 could expect to score twice, player 2 could expect to score three times, and player 3 could expect to score once. To make the game fair, you could give 3 points to player 1 if the spinner lands on 1, 2 points to player 2 if the spinner lands on 2, and 6 points to player 3 if the spinner lands on 3. In 12 spins, player 1 could expect to score four times for a total of $4 \times 3 = 12$ points, player 2 could expect to score six times for a total of $6 \times 2 = 12$ points, and player 3 could expect to score twice for a total of $2 \times 6 = 12$ points.

# Theoretical Probabilities

In this investigation, experimental and theoretical probabilities are formally introduced in the context of drawing colored blocks from a bucket. This is the first time students are directly asked to find and compare experimental and theoretical probabilities. This investigation is more teacher-directed than the others in the unit. The block-drawing activities are intended to be facilitated by the teacher because the goal is to help students carefully develop definitions of experimental and theoretical probability.

In Problem 4.1, Predicting to Win, students gather data to determine the probabilities of drawing blocks of various colors from a bucket. After finding these experimental probabilities, they inspect the blocks and compute the theoretical probabilities. The goals of this whole-class activity are to have students form a working definition of *probability* and to begin to contrast theoretical and experimental probabilities. In Problem 4.2, Drawing More Blocks, they reverse these steps—computing the theoretical probabilities first and then conducting an experiment to find experimental probabilities. In Problem 4.3, Winning the Bonus Prize, students consider the possible results when a block is drawn from each of two containers. In this situation, the possible outcomes are pairs, and students must make an organized list to compute the theoretical probabilities.

## Mathematical and Problem-Solving Goals

■ *To understand the two ways to obtain probabilities: by gathering data from experiments (experimental probability) and by analyzing possible and favorable outcomes (theoretical probability)*

■ *To understand the relationship between experimental and theoretical probabilities: when an experimental probability is based on a large number of trials, it is a good estimate of the theoretical probability*

■ *To develop strategies for finding theoretical probabilities, such as making an organized list of all possible outcomes*

■ *To develop an understanding of the word* random

| Materials | | |
|---|---|---|
| **Problem** | **For students** | **For the teacher** |
| **All** | Calculators | Transparencies 4.1 to 4.3 (optional) |
| **4.1** | | Opaque bucket or bag filled with 9 red blocks, 6 yellow blocks, and 3 blue blocks (substitute other colors or objects if necessary) |
| **4.2** | Opaque container filled with 4 red blocks, 3 yellow blocks, and 1 blue block (optional, 1 per group; substitute other colors or objects if necessary) | Opaque bucket or bag filled with 4 red blocks, 3 yellow blocks, and 1 blue block (substitute other colors or objects if necessary) |
| **4.3** | Opaque containers filled with 1 red block, 1 yellow block, and 1 blue block (optional, 2 per group; substitute other colors or objects if necessary) | Two opaque containers, each containing 1 red block, 1 yellow block, and 1 blue block (substitute other colors or objects if necessary) |

Student Pages 29–41     Teaching the Investigation 41a–41e

# Theoretical Probabilities

**I**n the last three investigations, you worked with problems involving the chances that a particular event would occur. Another word for chance is *probability*. So far, you have determined probabilities by doing experiments and collecting data. For example, you flipped a coin many times and found that the probability of getting a head is $\frac{1}{2}$. You also discovered that the more trials that were done, the better the probabilities that you found could predict future outcomes.

The results of the coin-flipping experiment probably did not surprise you. You already knew that when a coin is flipped there are two possible outcomes—heads and tails—and that each outcome is equally likely. In fact, you could have found the probability of getting a head by *analyzing* the possible outcomes instead of by *experimenting*. Since there are two equally likely outcomes, and one of these outcomes is a head, the probability of getting a head is 1 out of 2, or $\frac{1}{2}$.

In this investigation, you will look at some other situations in which you can find the probabilities both by experimenting and by analyzing the possible outcomes.

## 4.1 Predicting to Win

In the last 5 minutes of the Gee Whiz Everyone Wins! television game show, all the members of the studio audience are called to the stage to select a block randomly from a bucket containing an unknown number of red, yellow, and blue blocks. Before drawing, each contestant is asked to predict the color of the block he or she will draw. If the guess is correct, the contestant wins a prize. After each draw, the block is put back into the bucket.

---

# Predicting to Win

## At a Glance

***Grouping:***
***Whole Class, then Pairs***

### Launch

- Introduce the block-guessing game, and talk about whether there is an advantage to going first or last.

- Discuss why the blocks must be returned to the container after each draw.

### Explore

- As a class, collect data by having each student predict a color, draw a block, and replace the block.

- Assign the follow-up to be done in pairs.

### Summarize

- Revisit the question of whether there is an advantage to going first or last.

- Discuss the follow-up questions.

## Assignment Choices

ACE questions 1, 2, 4, and unassigned choices from earlier problems

## Think about this!

**S**uppose you are a member of the audience. Is there an advantage to being called to the stage first? Is there an advantage to being called last? Why?

### Problem 4.1

Play the block-guessing game with your class. Your teacher will act as the host of the game show, and you and your classmates will be the contestants. Keep a record of the number of times each color is drawn. Play the game until you think you can predict with certainty the chances of each color being drawn.

**A.** In your class experiment, how many blue blocks were drawn? Red blocks? Yellow blocks? What was the total number of blocks drawn?

**B.** The probability of drawing a red block can be written as P(red). Find all three probabilities based on the data you collected in your experiment.

P(red) =          P(yellow) =          P(blue) =

Now, your teacher will dump out the blocks so you can see them.

**C.** How many of the blocks are red? Yellow? Blue? How many blocks are there altogether?

**D.** Find the fraction of the total blocks that are red, the fraction that are yellow, and the fraction that are blue.

## Answers to Problem 4.1

A. Answers will vary.

B. Answers will vary. If you have 25 students, and they drew 15 red blocks altogether, the experimental probability of drawing a red block would be $\frac{15}{25}$ or 60%.

C. 9 red; 6 yellow; 3 blue; 18 altogether

D. The fraction that are red is $\frac{9}{18} = \frac{1}{2}$. The fraction that are yellow is $\frac{6}{18} = \frac{1}{3}$. The fraction that are blue is $\frac{3}{18} = \frac{1}{6}$.

### Problem 4.1 Follow-Up

The probabilities you computed in part B are called **experimental probabilities** because you found them by experimenting. The fractions you found in part D are called **theoretical probabilities.** You find theoretical probabilities by analyzing the possible outcomes rather than by experimenting.

If all the outcomes of an action are equally likely, then the theoretical probability of an event is computed with this formula:

$$\frac{\text{number of favorable outcomes}}{\text{number of possible outcomes}}$$

where *favorable outcomes* are the outcomes in which you are interested.

For example, if you want to find the probability of drawing a red block, a red block is a favorable outcome. If a bucket has a total of six blocks, and two of the blocks are red, the theoretical probability of drawing a red block is $\frac{2}{6}$.

6 possible outcomes (blocks)
2 favorable outcomes (red blocks)

Theoretical probability
of drawing a red block $= \frac{2}{6}$

1. Compare the *experimental probabilities* you found in part B to the *theoretical probabilities* you found in part D. Are the experimental and theoretical probabilities for each color of block close to each other? Do you think they should be close? Why or why not?

2. **a.** When you drew a block from the bucket, did each *block* have an equally likely chance of being chosen? Explain.

   **b.** When you drew a block from the bucket, did each *color* have an equally likely chance of being chosen? Explain.

3. Look back at the "Think about this!" on page 30. Is there an advantage to being the first person to draw from the bucket? To being the last person to draw?

4. In the Gee Whiz Everyone Wins! game show, contestants select a block randomly from the bucket. What do you think *random* means?

**Investigation 4: Theoretical Probabilities** **31**

## Answers to Problem 4.1 Follow-Up

1. The probabilities should be close, and we should expect them to be close. For example, since 9 of the 18 blocks are red, we should expect to choose red about half the time. For a small number of trials, the numbers might not be extremely close. If we did many more trials, we would expect the numbers to be very close.

2. a. yes; Since the blocks can't be seen and all of them are the same size and shape, all have the same chance of being drawn.

   b. no; The number of blocks is different for each color. Since there are more red blocks than blue blocks in the bucket, for example, there is a greater chance of drawing red than blue.

3–4. See page 41d.

# Drawing More Blocks

### Launch

■ Explain that students will first compute the theoretical probability of each color in the bucket and then find experimental probabilities.

### Explore

■ As a whole class, or in groups, analyze the contents of the container and find the theoretical probabilities.

■ Conduct an experiment to find experimental probabilities.

### Summarize

■ Compare the theoretical results with the experimental results.

■ Review the definitions of experimental and theoretical probabilities.

---

**4.2 Drawing More Blocks**

Your teacher put eight blocks in a bucket. All the blocks are the same size. Three are yellow, four are red, and one is blue.

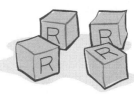

### Problem 4.2

**A.** When you draw a block from the bucket, are the chances equally likely that it will be yellow, red, or blue? Explain your answer.

**B.** What is the total number of blocks? How many blocks of each color are there?

**C.** What is the *theoretical probability* of drawing a blue block? A yellow block? A red block? Explain how you found each answer.

Now, as a class or in groups, take turns drawing a block from the bucket. After each draw, return the block to the bucket. Keep a record of the blocks that are drawn. If you work in a group, take turns drawing blocks until you have 40 trials.

**D.** Based on your data, what is the *experimental probability* of drawing a blue block? A yellow block? A red block?

**E.** Compare the theoretical probabilities you found in part C to the experimental probabilities you found in part D. Are the probabilities for each color close? Are they the same? If not, why not?

### ▨ Problem 4.2 Follow-Up

Suppose you and your classmates each took three turns drawing a block from the bucket, replacing the block each time, and then used the large amount of data you collected to find new experimental probabilities for drawing each color. You found the theoretical probability of drawing each color in part C. Do you think these new experimental probabilities would be closer to the theoretical probabilities than the experimental probabilities you found in part D were? Explain your reasoning.

---

### Assignment Choices

ACE questions 3, 5, 6, and unassigned choices from earlier problems

### Answers to Problem 4.2

A. No, because the number of blocks is different for each different color.

B. There are eight blocks—three yellow blocks, four red blocks, and one blue block.

C. To find the theoretical probability for a color, divide the number of blocks of that color by the total number of blocks. So, P(blue) = $\frac{1}{8}$, P(yellow) = $\frac{3}{8}$, and P(red) = $\frac{4}{8}$ = $\frac{1}{2}$.

D. Answers will vary.

E. The experimental probabilities will probably be fairly close to the theoretical probabilities. They are probably not the same, because it is unlikely the colors were drawn in the exact ratio in which they were in the bucket.

### 4.3 Winning the Bonus Prize

All the winners from the Gee Whiz Everyone Wins! game show get an opportunity to compete for a bonus prize. Each winner draws one block from each of two bags, both of which contain one red, one yellow, and one blue block. The contestant must predict which color she or he will draw from each of the two bags. If the prediction is correct, the contestant wins a $10,000 bonus prize!

Bag 1                    Bag 2

---

#### Problem 4.3

What are a contestant's chances of winning?

Conduct an experiment to help you answer this question. Keep track of the pairs of colors that are drawn, and make sure you collect enough data to give you good estimates of the probability of drawing each pair. Remember, contestants must guess the color of the block they will pick from each bag. That means you will have to count (a blue from bag 1, a red from bag 2) as a different pair from (a red from bag 1, a blue from bag 2).

**A.** Based on your experiment, what are a contestant's chances of winning?

**B.** List all the possible pairs that can be drawn from the bags. Are each of these pairs equally likely? Explain your answer.

**C.** What is the theoretical probability of each pair being drawn? Explain your answer.

**D.** How do the theoretical probabilities compare with your experimental probabilities? Explain any differences.

---

**Investigation 4: Theoretical Probabilities**  **33**

## At a Glance

**Grouping:**
*Whole Class or Groups*

### Launch

- Introduce the bonus game, making sure students understand how the situation differs from the previous problems.

- Record students' predictions about a contestant's probability of winning.

### Explore

- Have students experiment to find a contestant's probability of winning.

- Let students work on the rest of the problem and the follow-up.

### Summarize

- Discuss the problem and the follow-up.

- Review the differences between the outcomes in Problems 4.1 and 4.2 and the outcomes in this problem.

## Answer to Problem 4.2 Follow-Up

See page 41d.

## Answers to Problem 4.3

A. Answers will vary but should be near the theoretical probability of $\frac{1}{9}$ or 11%.

B. There are nine possible pairs: RR, RY, RB, YR, YY, YB, BR, BY, and BB. Each pair is equally likely.

C. The theoretical probability of each pair being drawn is $\frac{1}{9}$.

D. Answers will vary. If they are not close, students should realize that it is because they did not perform enough trials.

## Assignment Choices

ACE questions 7–9 (7 is a good class-discussion question) and unassigned choices from earlier problems

■ **Problem 4.3 Follow-Up**

Suppose you are a contestant on the show, and you have already won a mountain bike, a fantastic portable CD player, a vacation to Hawaii, and a one-year supply of Glimmer toothpaste. You have just played the bonus round and lost, but the host makes the following offer: you can draw from the two bags again, but this time you do not need to predict the color. If the two colors match, you will win $5000. If the two colors do not match, you must return all the prizes you have won. Would you accept this offer? Explain

## Answer to Problem 4.3 Follow-Up

Contestants should think twice before playing this game. A contestant wins by choosing the combination RR, YY, or BB, so P(match) = $\frac{3}{9}$ and P(no match) = $\frac{6}{9}$. Students may argue that having a 1 in 3 chance of winning $5000 is worth the risk of losing the prizes won so far.

As you work on these ACE questions, use your calculator whenever you need it.

# Applications

**1.** A bucket contains one green block, one red block, and two yellow blocks.

   **a.** Find the theoretical probability of choosing each color.

   P(green) = _____    P(yellow) = _____    P(red) = _____

   **b.** Find the sum of the probabilities in part a.

   **c.** What is the probability of *not* drawing a red block? Explain how you found your answer.

   **d.** What do you get when you add the probability of *getting* a red to the probability of *not getting* a red?

   **e.** What happens to the probability of drawing a red block if the number of blocks of each color is doubled?

   **f.** What happens to the probability of drawing a red block if two more blocks of each color are added to the original bucket?

   **g.** How many blocks of which colors would you have to add to the original bucket to make the probability of drawing a red block $\frac{1}{2}$?

---

**Investigation 4: Theoretical Probabilities** | **35**

## Answers

### Applications

**1a.** P(green) = $\frac{1}{4}$, P(yellow) = $\frac{2}{4}$ = $\frac{1}{2}$, P(red) = $\frac{1}{4}$

**1b.** $\frac{1}{4} + \frac{1}{2} + \frac{1}{4} = 1$

**1c.** $\frac{3}{4}$; Three out of the four blocks are not red.

**1d.** $\frac{1}{4} + \frac{3}{4} = 1$

**1e.** The probability doesn't change. There would be eight blocks in all, and two would be red, so the probability of getting red is still $\frac{2}{8}$ = $\frac{1}{4}$.

**1f.** There would be ten blocks in the bucket, and three would be red, so the probability of drawing a red block would be $\frac{3}{10}$.

**1g.** Possible answer: You could add two red blocks. Then, three out of six blocks, or $\frac{1}{2}$, would be red.

**2a.** $\frac{3}{3} = 1$

**2b.** $\frac{0}{3} = 0$

**2c.** $\frac{0}{3} = 0$

**3a.** P(green) = $\frac{12}{25}$,
P(purple) = $\frac{6}{25}$,
P(orange) = $\frac{2}{25}$,
P(yellow) = $\frac{5}{25}$

**3b.** $\frac{12}{25} + \frac{6}{25} + \frac{2}{25} + \frac{5}{25} = 1$

**3c.** P(green) = 48%,
P(purple) = 24%,
P(orange) = 8%,
P(yellow) = 20%

**3d.** 48% + 24% + 8% + 20% = 100%

**3e.** 1 or 100%.

**(Teaching Tip:** If the possible outcomes of an action do not overlap and account for everything that might happen, then the sum of the probabilities of the outcomes will be 1. Throughout the remainder of this unit, you might ask students questions to help them see that this is true.)

**4a.** Possible answer: The *probability* of something is the chance that it will occur. It is an estimate of behavior over the long run.

**4b.** Possible answer: Probabilities are important in situations in which predicting the future and making decisions based on predictions are important. Some examples are the weather (like rain and tornadoes), health (like the chances of getting a disease), and games of chance (like lotteries and bingo).

---

**2.** A bag contains exactly three blocks, all blue.

   **a.** What is the probability of drawing a blue block?

   **b.** What is the probability of *not* drawing a blue block?

   **c.** What is the probability of drawing a yellow block?

**3.** A bubble-gum machine contains 25 gum balls. There are 12 green, 6 purple, 2 orange, and 5 yellow gum balls.

   **a.** Find the theoretical probability of getting each color.

   P(green) = _____        P(purple) = _____

   P(orange) = _____       P(yellow) = _____

   **b.** What is the sum of the probabilities for all the possible colors?

   P(green) + P(purple) + P(orange) + P(yellow) = _____

   **c.** Write each of the probabilities in part a as a percent.

   P(green) = _____        P(purple) = _____

   P(orange) = _____       P(yellow) = _____

   **d.** What is the sum of all the probabilities as a percent?

   **e.** What do you think the sum of the probabilities for all possible outcomes must be for any situation?

**4. a.** What do you think the word *probability* means?

   **b.** Describe some situations in which probability is important.

**5. a.** If two people do an experiment to estimate the probability of a particular event occurring, will they get the same result? Explain why or why not.

**b.** If two people analyze a situation to find the theoretical probability of an event occurring, and each person does a correct analysis, will they get the same result? Explain why or why not.

**c.** If one person uses an experiment to estimate the probability of an event occurring and another person analyzes the situation to find the theoretical probability of the event occurring, will they get the same result? Explain why or why not.

## Connections

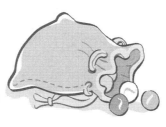

**6.** A bag contains several marbles. Some are red, some are white, and some are blue. Carlos counted the marbles and found that the theoretical probability of drawing a red marble is $\frac{1}{6}$ and the theoretical probability of drawing a white marble is $\frac{1}{3}$.

**a.** What is the smallest number of marbles that could be in the bag?

**b.** Could the bag contain 48 marbles? If so, how many of each color must it contain?

**c.** If the bag contains 4 red marbles and 8 white marbles, how many blue marbles must it contain?

**d.** How can you tell what the probability of a drawing a blue marble is?

**5a.** not necessarily; Their experiments will probably give them different results, but their results should be close—especially if they each conducted a large number of trials.

**5b.** yes; The theoretical probability in a given situation is the same no matter who finds it.

**5c.** They probably won't get the same results but their results will probably be close, especially if the experimental probability is based on a large number of trials.

### *Connections*

**6a.** Since the probability of drawing a red marble is $\frac{1}{6}$, there must be at least 6 marbles in the bag.

**6b.** yes; Possible answer: Let's assume the bag contains 48 marbles. Since the probability of drawing red is $\frac{1}{6}$, then $\frac{1}{6}$ of the proposed 48 marbles—or 8 marbles—would be red. Since $\frac{1}{3}$ of the 48 marbles must be white, 16 would be white. This gives us a total of 24 marbles, so the other 24 marbles would be blue. Since we get whole numbers of marbles when we do this division, the bag could contain 48 marbles.

**6c.** Possible answer: Since $\frac{1}{3}$ of the marbles in the bag are white, and 8 marbles are white, we need to answer this question: $\frac{1}{3}$ of what number equals 8? The answer is 24. Since 4 marbles are red and 8 are white, there are 12 blue marbles in the bag.

**6d.** See page 41d.

**7a.** From counting, we know there are 28 people in the class. Since picking each person is equally likely, and 4 of the 28 have first names that begin with J, the probability is $\frac{4}{28} = \frac{1}{7}$.

**7b.** There are 17 names that begin with a letter from G through S, so the probability of selecting a student in this range is $\frac{17}{28}$.

**7c.** $\frac{1}{28}$

**7d.** The class now has 30 students, and since there are still only 4 whose names begin with J, the new probability is $\frac{4}{30} = \frac{2}{15}$.

**7.** Katherine's class made this line plot of the first letters in the first names of all the students in her class.

```
                        X
                        X                   X
    X                   X     X     X     X X
    X X   X X X X X     X X X X X   X   X X X       X   X X
    ─────────────────────────────────────────────────────────
    A B C D E F G H I J K L M N O P Q R S T U V W X Y Z
                              Letter
```

**a.** If you randomly select a student from Katherine's class, what is the probability you will choose someone whose first name begins with J?

**b.** If you randomly select a student from Katherine's class, what is the probability you will choose someone whose first name begins with a letter that occurs after F in the alphabet, but before T?

**c.** If you randomly select a student from Katherine's class, what is the probability that you will choose Katherine?

**d.** Suppose two more people joined the class, Melvin and Theo. Now if you randomly select a student from the class, what is the probability you will choose someone whose first name begins with J?

**8.** Suppose you were to spin this spinner and then roll this six-sided number cube.

**a.** Make an organized list of the possible outcomes of a spin of the spinner and a roll of the number cube. For example, the outcome that is showing is this:

| Spinner | Number cube |
|---------|-------------|
| 2 | 2 |

**b.** What is the probability you would get a 2 on both the number cube and the spinner? Explain your reasoning.

**c.** What is the probability you would get a *factor* of 2 on both the number cube and the spinner?

**d.** What is the probability you would get a *multiple* of 2 on both the number cube and the spinner?

# Extensions

**9.** The cook in the Casimer Middle School cafeteria is in a bad mood! When Jonalyn went through the lunch line, she tried to tell the cook what she wanted, but the cook just mumbled, "Appreciate what you get!" Jonalyn thinks some of the things on the menu are really gross. Her favorite lunch is a grilled cheese sandwich, carrots, and a chocolate chip cookie.

**8a.**

| Spinner | Number cube |
|---------|-------------|
| 1 | 1 |
| 1 | 2 |
| 1 | 3 |
| 1 | 4 |
| 1 | 5 |
| 1 | 6 |
| 2 | 1 |
| 2 | 2 |
| 2 | 3 |
| 2 | 4 |
| 2 | 5 |
| 2 | 6 |

**8b.** Since (2, 2) is one of 12 equally likely possibilities, the probability is $\frac{1}{12}$.

**8c.** Since the factors of 2 are 1 and 2, the only possibilities are (1, 1), (1, 2), (2, 1), and (2, 2). Thus there are 4 ways out of 12 equally likely outcomes, so the probability is $\frac{4}{12} = \frac{1}{3}$.

**8d.** The multiples of 2 in the data are 2, 4, and 6, so the only possibilities are (2, 2), (2, 4), and (2, 6). Thus there are 3 ways out of 12 equally likely outcomes, so the probability is $\frac{3}{12} = \frac{1}{4}$.

## Extensions

**9a.** See below right.

**9b.** The probability of Jonalyn getting her favorite lunch is $\frac{1}{12}$. Since the cook is not paying any attention to how she puts the lunches together, and there are an equal number of each kind of sandwich, vegetable, and cookie, each of the 12 combinations is equally likely.

**9c.** The probability of Jonalyn getting at least one of her favorite things is $\frac{10}{12}$. Only 2 of the 12 combinations of items don't contain at least one of her favorite things.

**10.** Answers will vary. If students conduct enough trials, the two types of probability should be close.

Lunch at Casimer consists of one sandwich, one vegetable, and one cookie. The cook has an equal number of each kind of sandwich, vegetable, and cookie. She is not paying any attention to how she puts the lunches together.

**a.** How many different lunches are possible? Explain your answer.

**b.** What is the probability that Jonalyn will get her favorite lunch? Explain your reasoning.

**c.** What is the probability that Jonalyn will get at least *one* of her favorite things? Explain your reasoning.

**10.** Make up a bag containing 12 objects—such as blocks or marbles—of the same size and shape. Use three or four different colors.

**a.** Describe the contents of your bag.

**b.** Determine the *theoretical probability* of drawing each color by analyzing the bag's contents.

**c.** Conduct an experiment to determine the *experimental probability* of drawing each color. Carefully describe how you did your experiment and recorded your results.

**d.** How do the two types of probability you found compare?

**9a.** There are 12 different possible lunches.

| Sandwich | Vegetable | Cookie |
|---|---|---|
| Grilled cheese | Carrots | Chocolate chip |
| Grilled cheese | Carrots | Oatmeal |
| Grilled cheese | Spinach | Chocolate chip |
| Grilled cheese | Spinach | Oatmeal |
| Hamburger | Carrots | Chocolate chip |
| Hamburger | Carrots | Oatmeal |
| Hamburger | Spinach | Chocolate chip |
| Hamburger | Spinach | Oatmeal |
| Turkey | Carrots | Chocolate chip |
| Turkey | Carrots | Oatmeal |
| Turkey | Spinach | Chocolate chip |
| Turkey | Spinach | Oatmeal |

# Mathematical Reflections

In this investigation, you studied a new way to find probabilities. You now have two ways to get information about the chances, or probability, that something will occur. You can design an experiment and collect data (to find experimental probabilities), or you can think about a situation, analyzing the outcomes carefully to see exactly what might happen (to find theoretical probabilities). These questions will help you summarize what you have learned:

**1** How can you find the experimental probability of an event? Why is this called an *experimental probability?*

**2** How can you find the theoretical probability of an event? Why is this called a *theoretical probability?*

**3** When you tossed coins to figure out which cereal Kalvin would have for breakfast, you found experimental probabilities by counting heads and tails. You might have noticed that the more trials you did, the closer your experimental probability came to the theoretical probability of $\frac{1}{2}$. Do you think that conducting more trials will always bring your experimental probability closer to the theoretical probability? Why or why not?

**4** Think of some situations in which it would be easier to find theoretical probabilities than experimental probabilities. Explain your reasoning.

**5** Think of some situations in which it would be easier to find experimental probabilities than theoretical probabilities. Explain your reasoning.

Think about your answers to these questions, discuss your ideas with other students and your teacher, and then write a summary of your findings in your journal.

## Tips for the Linguistically Diverse Classroom

**Original Rebus** The Original Rebus technique is described in detail in *Getting to Know Connected Mathematics*. Students make a copy of the text before it is discussed. During discussion, they generate their own rebuses for words they do not understand as the words are made comprehensible through pictures, objects, or demonstrations. Example: Question 1—a key term for which students may make a rebus is *experimental probability* (a coin being tossed in the air and a sheet of paper with tally marks under the headings "heads" and "tails").

## Possible Answers

**1.** If you experiment to figure out the probability of an event, such as drawing a blue block from a bag of blocks, you can carry out a series of trials, tally your results, and write the probability like this:

$$\frac{\text{number of times you drew a blue block}}{\text{number of times you drew a block}}$$

This is called an *experimental probability* because it is based on experiments.

**2.** If you analyze a situation by thinking about the range of possible outcomes (when the outcomes are equally likely), you can list all the possible outcomes and find the probability of an event, such as drawing a blue block, like this:

$$\frac{\text{number of blue blocks in the bag}}{\text{number of blocks in the bag}}$$

This is called the *theoretical probability* because it is based on analyzing a situation to determine what should happen in theory.

**3.** Generally speaking, yes. If the experiment is conducted without bias, the more data you collect, the better you will be able to predict what will happen over the long run.

**4.** A coin toss, a roll of a pair of number cubes, and a spin of a spinner are situations in which the theoretical probabilities are obvious and therefore easier to find than experimental probabilities.

**5.** See page 41d.

# TEACHING THE INVESTIGATION

## 4.1 • Predicting to Win

Throughout this unit, students are asked questions that lead them to realize that the more information they have, the better their predictions will be. Another way to state this is that the more trials an experimental probability is based on, the better estimate it will be of the theoretical probability. This concept is developed further through the work in this investigation.

### Launch

With your students, read the opening paragraphs of Investigation 4—which summarize some very important ideas in this unit—then tell the story of the game show.

Talk about the questions in the "Think about this!" box on page 30. You might be surprised that some students see no advantage to going last.

> We are going to play this game as a class. I will be the host, and you will be the contestants. You will take turns drawing from the container. We need to keep careful track of the outcome of each draw.
>
> After each turn, we will return the container to its original state by replacing the block and then mixing the blocks. Why do we need to do this?

Help students to recognize that if the blocks are not returned to the container, the probabilities will change with each draw because the blocks in the container will be different.

### Explore

Ask students one at a time for their guess, then let them draw out and replace one block. Have one student keep track of the colors that are drawn by making a line plot or a chart with tally marks at the board. You may want to provide small prizes for students who guess correctly. You may choose to do both the problem and the follow-up as teacher-directed, whole-class explorations or to assign the follow-up questions to be done in pairs.

### Summarize

Ask students once again whether there is an advantage to going first or going last. After having played the game, students should recognize that there is an advantage to going last, because you have more information about what is in the bucket—and you can find better experimental probabilities with more information. Knowing the probabilities does not assure that you will guess correctly, but a guess based on good experimental probabilities can be more predictive of what will happen over time.

Discuss all of the follow-up questions during the summary.

# 4.2 • Drawing More Blocks

This problem reinforces the ideas of theoretical and experimental probabilities developed in Problem 4.1. This time, students compute the theoretical probabilities first and then find experimental probabilities.

## Launch

You can do this activity either as a class or in groups, with each group having a bucket of blocks.

> I am putting three yellow blocks, four red blocks, and one blue block in this bucket. In this problem, you will first compute the theoretical probability of drawing each color from the bucket. Then, you will find experimental probabilities.

## Explore

Either do the problem as a whole class or let the students work in groups of four. If students work in groups, each group will need a container of blocks. Each student in the group should draw 10 times, replacing the block each time. Groups should organize their data, write both experimental and theoretical probabilities, and discuss the follow-up. Circulate and make sure students are not biasing the outcome by the way they draw the blocks.

## Summarize

Review the answers to the problem and the follow-up question. Review the definitions of experimental and theoretical probabilities, and discuss how they are related.

The follow-up asks whether conducting more trials would bring the students' experimental probabilities closer to the theoretical probabilities. If time allows and your students are interested, give it a try and find out.

# 4.3 • Winning the Bonus Prize

This problem introduces a new level of complexity. In this problem, one block is drawn from each of two bags, so an outcome consists of two blocks, not one.

## Launch

Be sure students understand how this game differs from the two earlier games. This activity works well both as a whole-class experiment or in groups, with each group having two containers of blocks.

> What do you think are the chances of a contestant winning this game?

Record students' predictions on the board. Ask some students how they came up with their predictions.

## Explore

Students should gather the experimental data and answer part A before they move on to the theoretical analysis. Allow them to experiment and decide for themselves when they have enough data to make a good estimate of a contestant's chances of winning. After they complete the experiment, have them work on the rest of the problem and the follow-up questions. If students do the activity in groups, pool the class's data before students answer part A.

Students may have trouble organizing the pairs of outcomes in part B; you may need to help them make an organized list. Here is one way to organize the information.

|  |  | Bag 1 |  |  |
|---|---|:---:|:---:|:---:|
|  |  | R | Y | B |
|  | R | RR | RY | RB |
| Bag 2 | Y | YR | YY | YB |
|  | B | BR | BY | BB |

Discuss how students know when they have found all the possible outcomes.

## Summarize

Discuss the problem and the follow-up. This problem offers another opportunity to help students see the difference between experimental relative frequencies as estimates of probabilities and probabilities arrived at by analyzing all possible outcomes and assigning probabilities based on that analysis. When the number of trials is large, these two probabilities should be close. Have a class discussion about the kinds of outcomes in Problems 4.1 and 4.2 and the kind of outcome in this problem. The outcomes in Problems 4.1 and 4.2 are single values (red, blue, or yellow). The outcomes here are pairs—for example, (red, yellow), (red, red), or (red, blue). You might describe these outcomes as "two-stage" outcomes to help students see the difference.

---

### For the Teacher: Revisiting Problem 2.2

Now that students have learned to analyze outcomes, you may want to return to the coin-tossing game from Problem 2.2 and ask them to think about how to make this game fair.

Students often suggest changing the rules. For example, they may suggest letting one player score on two or more heads and the other player score on two or more tails. If no student mentions adjusting the point scheme, ask:

*Can we make the game fair by changing the number of points scored by each player?*

Some students may see that giving one player 3 points for tossing three matching coins and the other player 1 point for tossing two matching coins makes the game fair. You can demonstrate this with an example.

*If each player takes eight turns, how many times would each expect to score?*

The player who scores on three of a kind would score about twice. The player who scores on a pair would score about six times.

---

> *If each player got 1 point each time he or she scored, what could we expect the score to be after eight turns?*

It would be 6 to 2, in favor of the player who scores on pairs.

> *How many points would we have to give the "three of a kind" player for the total expected points to be the same as for the "pairs" player?*

To make 6 points—the same as the other player—we would have to give the "three of a kind" player 3 points per score.

# Additional Answers

## Answers to Problem 4.1 Follow-Up

3. There is no advantage to going first. There is an advantage to going last, because you have more information about what is in the bucket.

4. Possible answer: *Random* means that the contestants' picks are based entirely on chance, or that each block in the bucket has an equally likely chance of being picked.

### For the Teacher: Random

The word *random* is used in different ways at different times. In this situation, *random* means that contestants select blocks in a way that does not bias the result of the draw. For example, the blocks may be shaken up or the participant may be blindfolded. We are not expecting a precise definition of the word at this level; we just want to raise the issue because students are bound to hear the word used in other contexts.

## Answer to Problem 4.2 Follow-Up

The new experimental probabilities would be based on many more trials and would probably be closer to the theoretical probabilities than our original experimental probabilities were.

## ACE Answers

### Connections

**6d.** Possible answer: You could tell by adding the other two probabilities (of red and white) and subtracting the result from 1: $\frac{1}{6} + \frac{1}{3} = \frac{3}{6}$, and $1 - \frac{3}{6} = \frac{3}{6} = \frac{1}{2}$. So the probability of drawing a blue marble is $\frac{1}{2}$.

## Mathematical Reflections

**5.** There are many situations in which there is no accessible method for finding theoretical probabilities; for example, the tossing of marshmallows. When physicians are testing a new drug on patients, they are finding experimental probabilities. When market researchers survey people to find out what products they might buy, they are finding experimental probabilities.

# Analyzing Games of Chance

**T**his investigation involves a two-team game.

In Problem 5.1, Playing Roller Derby, students play and analyze a game called Roller Derby. To play the game, each team places 12 markers in any way they choose on a game board with columns numbered from 1 to 12. The teams then take turns rolling two number cubes and removing a marker from the column corresponding to the sum of the cubes. The first team to remove all of their markers wins.

After playing the game, students list all the possible outcomes, or number pairs, and use the list to devise strategies for winning the game. This is the largest listing problem of the unit, and many students may need your guidance to systematically list all 36 possible pairs. A chart of all the outcomes provides a rich connection to factors and multiples and to evens and odds.

## Mathematical and Problem-Solving Goals

- **To understand the two ways to obtain probabilities: by gathering data from experiments (experimental probability) and by analyzing possible and favorable outcomes (theoretical probability)**

- **To develop strategies for finding theoretical probabilities, such as making an organized list of all possible outcomes**

- **To gain a better understanding of what it means for events to be equally likely in situations in which individual outcomes are combined to obtain the events of interest**

| Materials | | |
|-----------|--------|---------------|
| **Problem** | **For students** | **For the teacher** |
| **5.1** | Calculators, Labsheet 5.1 (1 per pair), number cubes (2 per pair), game markers (counters, buttons, or other small objects; 12 per pair) | Transparency 5.1 (optional), transparency of Labsheet 5.1, game markers, number cubes (2 cubes of different colors, optional) |

**Student Pages 42–48**     **Teaching the Investigation 48a–48e**

# Playing Roller Derby

# Analyzing Games of Chance

**H**ave you ever figured out a strategy for winning a game? In this activity, you will play a two-team game called Roller Derby. As you play, think about strategies for winning and the probabilities associated with those strategies.

### 5.1 Playing Roller Derby

In a game of Roller Derby, two teams compete. Each team needs a game board with columns numbered 1 through 12, a pair of number cubes, and 12 markers (like pennies, buttons, or small blocks).

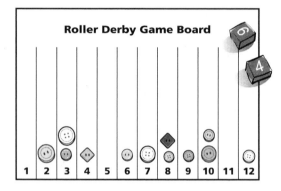

**Roller Derby Game Board**

**Roller Derby Rules**

1. Each team places its 12 markers into the columns in any way it chooses.
2. Each team rolls a number cube. The team with the highest roll goes first.
3. Teams take turns rolling the two number cubes and removing a marker from the column with the same number as the total shown on the cubes. If the column is empty, the team does not get to remove a marker.
4. The first team to remove all the markers from its board wins.

### Answer to Problem 5.1

The goal is not for students to come up with the one best strategy for placing the markers, but to realize that sums near the center (6, 7, and 8) are more likely to occur than sums at the ends. The actual analysis to find the one best placement is quite difficult; you could suggest it as a challenge problem for interested students.

### Problem 5.1

What is a good strategy for placing your markers in the 12 columns on the game board?

Play the game at least twice before answering this question. As you play, keep a record of the strategies you use.

### ▨ Problem 5.1 Follow-Up

**1. a.** Find a systematic way to list all the possible outcomes (number pairs) of rolling two number cubes and the sums for each of these outcomes. Analyze your list carefully before answering b–e.

**b.** What sums are possible when you roll two cubes?

**c.** Which sum or sums occur most often?

**d.** How many ways can you get a sum of 6? A sum of 2?

**e.** Are all the sums equally likely? Explain.

**2.** Now that you have analyzed the possible outcomes, do you have any new ideas for a strategy for winning Roller Derby? Explain. If time allows, play the game again using your new strategy.

## Answers to Problem 5.1 Follow-Up

1.  a.  See page 48c.

    b.  2, 3, 4, 5, 6, 7, 8, 9, 10, 11, and 12

    c.  See page 48c.

    d.  There are five ways to get a sum of 6 and one way to get a sum of 2.

    e.  no; Although each possible pair of numbers is equally likely, each sum is not. For example, there are three ways to get 4 and only one way to get 12, so you are more likely to get 4.

2.  See page 48d.

## Answers

### Applications

**1.** The probability that Eleanor will win is 0, and the probability that Carlos will win is 1. It is impossible to roll a sum of 1, so Carlos will eventually win.

**2.** $\frac{6}{36}$; Six out of the 36 possible outcomes are doubles.

### Connections

**3.** $\frac{2}{36} = \frac{1}{18}$

**4.** $\frac{3}{36} + \frac{2}{36} + \frac{1}{36} = \frac{6}{36} = \frac{1}{6}$

---

**Applications • Connections • Extensions**

As you work on these ACE questions, use your calculator whenever you need it.

# Applications

**1.** Eleanor is playing Roller Derby with Carlos. Eleanor placed all of her markers in column 1, and Carlos placed all of his markers in column 12. What is the probability that Eleanor will win? What is the probability that Carlos will win? Explain your reasoning.

**2.** When you play the game of Monopoly®, you sometimes end up in "jail." One way to get out of jail is to roll a double (two cubes that match). What is the probability of getting out of jail on your turn by rolling a double? Use your list of possible outcomes of rolling two number cubes to help you answer this question. Explain your reasoning.

# Connections

In 3–9, use your list of possible outcomes of rolling two number cubes to help you answer the question.

**3.** When two number cubes are rolled, what is the probability that their sum will be 3?

**4.** When two number cubes are rolled, what is the probability that their sum will be greater than 9?

**5.** When two number cubes are rolled, what is the probability that their sum will be a multiple of 4?

**6.** When two number cubes are rolled, what is the probability that their sum will be a common multiple of 2 and 3?

**7.** When two number cubes are rolled, what is the probability that their sum will be a prime number? Explain.

**8.** Which has a greater probability of being rolled on a pair of number cubes—a sum that is a factor of 6 or a sum that is a multiple of 6? Explain.

**9.** Humberto and Kate are playing a game called Odds and Evens. To play the game, they roll two number cubes. If the sum is odd, Humberto scores a point. If the sum is even, Kate scores a point. Is this a fair game of chance? Why or why not?

**10.** Suppose that Humberto and Kate play a game called Evens and Odds. (This game is similar to the game in question 9, except it involves *products* instead of *sums*.) To play the game, they roll two number cubes. If the product is odd, Kate scores a point. If the product is even, Humberto scores a point.

    **a.** Make an organized table of the possible products of two number cubes.

    **b.** What is the probability that Kate will win? What is the probability that Humberto will win? Explain your reasoning.

    **c.** Is this a fair game? If it is fair, explain why. If it is not fair, tell how you could change the points scored by each player so that it would be fair.

    **d.** What is the probability that the product rolled will be a prime number?

    **e.** What is the probability that the product rolled will be a factor of 30?

    **f.** What is the probability that the product rolled will be greater than 18?

**10a.** This table lists the possible products.

**Cube 2**

|  | 1 | 2 | 3 | 4 | 5 | 6 |
|---|---|---|---|---|---|---|
| **1** | 1 | 2 | 3 | 4 | 5 | 6 |
| **2** | 2 | 4 | 6 | 8 | 10 | 12 |
| **3** | 3 | 6 | 9 | 12 | 15 | 18 |
| **4** | 4 | 8 | 12 | 16 | 20 | 24 |
| **5** | 5 | 10 | 15 | 20 | 25 | 30 |
| **6** | 6 | 12 | 18 | 24 | 30 | 36 |

**Cube 1**

---

**5.** $\frac{3}{36} + \frac{5}{36} + \frac{1}{36} = \frac{9}{36} = \frac{1}{4}$

**6.** $\frac{5}{36} + \frac{1}{36} = \frac{6}{36} = \frac{1}{4}$

**7.** $\frac{15}{36}$; The possible prime sums are 2, 3, 5, 7, and 11. There is one way to get 2, two ways to get 3, four ways to get 5, six ways to get 7, and two ways to get 11, so there are 1 + 2 + 4 + 6 + 2 = 15 ways to get a prime number.

**8.** The probability of getting a sum that is a factor of 6 is greater. There are five ways to get 6, two ways to get 3, and one way to get 2, so the probability of getting a sum that is a factor of 6 is $\frac{8}{36}$. There are five ways to get 6 and one way to get 12, so the probability of getting a sum that is a multiple of 6 is $\frac{6}{36}$.

**9.** See page 48d.

**10a.** See below left.

**10b.** There are 1 + 2 + 2 + 1 + 2 + 1 = 9 ways to get an odd product, so the probability Kate will win is only $\frac{9}{36} = \frac{1}{4}$. There are 2 + 3 + 4 + 2 + 2 + 4 + 1 + 2 + 2 + 2 + 2 + 1 = 27 ways to get an even product, so the probability Humberto will win is $\frac{27}{36} = \frac{3}{4}$.

**10c.** This is not a fair game of chance, because Humberto has a better chance of winning than Kate. To make the game fair, you could give Kate 3 points each time she scores. This will mean that in a game of 12 rolls, Kate would expect to score 3 times for a total of 9 points. Humberto would expect to score 9 times for a total of 9 points.

**10d–f.** See page 48d.

**11a.** You could choose either spinner, because the probability of landing on pizza is $\frac{3}{12}$ on both spinners.

**11b.** Choose spinner A, because the probability for lasagna is $\frac{3}{12}$ on spinner A and $\frac{2}{12}$ on spinner B.

**11c.** Choose spinner B, because the probability for hot dogs is $\frac{2}{12}$ on spinner A and $\frac{3}{12}$ on spinner B.

**12.** See pages 48d and 48e.

**13.** This is not a fair game of chance. There are eight equally likely possibilities (HHH, HHT, HTT, TTT, TTH, THH, THT, and HTH), and only two are matches. Hence, the probability Fumi will get a point is only $\frac{2}{8}$, while the probability Alex will get a point is $\frac{6}{8}$. Alex has a better chance of winning.

**11.** The cooks at Kyla's school made the spinners shown below to help them determine the lunch menu. They let the students take turns spinning to determine the daily menu. In a–c, decide which spinner you would choose, and explain your reasoning.

**Spinner A**

**Spinner B**

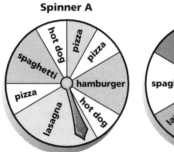
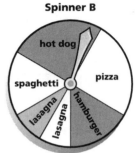

**a.** Your favorite lunch is pizza.

**b.** Your favorite lunch is lasagna.

**c.** Your favorite lunch is hot dogs.

**12.** Abigail and Christopher are playing a game with two coins. To play the game, they each flip a coin at the same time. If the two coins match, Christopher gets a point; if they do not match, Abigail gets a point. Is this a fair game of chance? Explain your reasoning.

**13.** Alex and Fumi are playing a game with three coins. To play the game, they flip all three coins at the same time. If the three coins match, Fumi gets a point. If they do not all match, Alex gets a point. Is this a fair game of chance? Explain your reasoning.

# Extensions

**14.** Make up three probability questions that can be answered by looking at your list of possible outcomes of rolling two number cubes. Then answer your own questions.

In 15–18, suppose Selina has just rolled three number cubes.

**15.** What is the probability that all three cubes match? Explain your reasoning.

**16.** What is the probability that the sum of the cubes is less than 5? Explain your reasoning.

**17.** What is the probability that the sum of the cubes is more than 2? Explain your reasoning.

**18.** What is the probability that the product of the cubes is prime? Explain your reasoning.

**Extensions**

**14.** Answers will vary.

**15.** $\frac{6}{216} = \frac{1}{36}$; We already know that there are 36 possible outcomes for two number cubes. If we combine each of these with 6 other outcomes for the third number cube, there will be $36 \times 6 = 216$ possible outcomes. Only 6 of these equally likely outcomes (111, 222, 333, 444, 555, and 666) are matches.

**16.** $\frac{4}{216} = \frac{1}{54}$; Only four possible outcomes produce a sum less than 5 (111, 112, 121, and 211).

**17.** 1; It is impossible to get a sum of less than 3 with three number cubes.

**18.** $\frac{9}{216} = \frac{1}{24}$; The only way to get a prime product is to get one prime number and two 1s. The nine ways to do this are 112, 121, 211, 113, 131, 311, 115, 151, and 511.

**1.** There are six possible outcomes: 1, 2, 3, 4, 5, and 6. Each is equally likely if the number cube is fair.

**2.** When you roll a pair of number cubes, 36 possible pairs can result: (1, 1), (1, 2), (1, 3), (1, 4), (1, 5), (1, 6), (2, 1), (2, 2), (2, 3), (2, 4), (2, 5), (2, 6), (3, 1), (3, 2), (3, 3), (3, 4), (3, 5), (3, 6), (4, 1), (4, 2), (4, 3), (4, 4), (4, 5), (4, 6), (5, 1), (5, 2), (5, 3), (5, 4), (5, 5), (5, 6), (6, 1), (6, 2), (6, 3), (6, 4), (6, 5), and (6, 6). Each pair is equally likely with a pair of fair number cubes.

**3.** There are 11 possible sums—2, 3, 4, 5, 6, 7, 8, 9, 10, 11, and 12—and they are not all equally likely. For example, there is only one way to get a sum of 2, but there are six ways to get a sum of 7. This means that the probability of a sum of 2 is only $\frac{1}{36}$, while the probability of a sum of 7 is $\frac{6}{36} = \frac{1}{6}$.

**4.** The probabilities of the sums when two number cubes are rolled are as follows: $P(2) = \frac{1}{36}$, $P(3) = \frac{2}{36}$, $P(4) = \frac{3}{36}$, $P(5) = \frac{4}{36}$, $P(6) = \frac{5}{36}$, $P(7) = \frac{6}{36}$, $P(8) = \frac{5}{36}$, $P(9) = \frac{4}{36}$, $P(10) = \frac{3}{36}$, $P(11) = \frac{2}{36}$, $P(12) = \frac{1}{36}$. The sum of these probabilities is 1, because the probabilities represent all that can happen when you roll two number cubes.

# Mathematical Reflections

**I**n this investigation, you played a game of chance that involved rolling a pair of number cubes and computing the sum of the cubes. These questions will help you summarize what you have learned:

**1** What are the possible outcomes when you roll one number cube? Is each of these outcomes equally likely?

**2** When you roll a pair of number cubes, how many different pairs of numbers can occur? Is each pair equally likely?

**3** In the Roller Derby game, you added the numbers on the faces of two number cubes. How many different sums were possible? Were they all equally likely? Explain.

**4** Suppose you roll two number cubes and add the results. What is the sum of the probabilities of all of these outcomes? Explain your answer.

Think about your answers to these questions, discuss your ideas with other students and your teacher, and then write a summary of your findings in your journal.

## Tips for the Linguistically Diverse Classroom

**Diagram Code** The Diagram Code technique is described in detail in *Getting to Know Connected Mathematics*. Students use a minimal number of words and drawings, diagrams, or symbols to respond to questions that require writing. Example: Question 1—A student might answer this question by listing 1, 2, 3, 4, 5, 6 with the label *equally likely* underneath.

# TEACHING THE INVESTIGATION

## 5.1 • Playing Roller Derby

This problem introduces a new way of collecting and analyzing data. Here we are not interested in individual outcomes—the separate numbers rolled on two number cubes—but an event, the sum of the numbers rolled on the pair of cubes.

### Launch

Discuss the directions for the game. A good way to illustrate the game is by displaying a transparency of Labsheet 5.1, putting markers in the columns randomly, and taking a few turns: toss a pair of number cubes, find the sum, and remove a marker (if present) from the corresponding column. Explain that if the column corresponding to a roll is empty, no marker is removed.

> What is your best guess at a strategy for placing your markers so that you will be able to remove them before your opponents remove their markers?

Here are some responses students have given.

- Rob suggested putting a marker in each column.

- Kari said that since you can't get a sum of 1, you should put a marker on every number except 1.

- Alaine thought it would be best to put all of the markers on 7.

- Paula suggested not putting any markers on high numbers.

Try to remain neutral when students make their initial suggestions. Playing the game will make them more aware of which strategies work and which do not.

Be sure students understand that the goal of the game is to eliminate all the markers. Divide the class into teams of two, and then pair teams to play against one another. Tell students to confer with their teammates, not their opponents, about how to arrange their 12 markers on the board.

### Explore

While students play the game, observe the strategies they are using and the knowledge they are displaying about sums of the numbers on the cubes.

### Summarize

After students have played the game a couple of times, ask them again about winning strategies.

> What was the first strategy your team used for placing markers in the 12 columns? Did you change your strategy the second time you played? Why or why not? If you played the game again, what strategy would you use? Why?

Give students some time to work on the follow-up questions and then discuss the answers as a class. Question 1 asks students to list all the possible outcomes of rolling two number cubes. The list should allow students to determine all the possible sums and to see all the ways each sum can occur.

What strategies did you use for making your list?

Some students may have found all the possible combinations by listing all the pairs with 1 first, all the pairs with 2 first, and so on. Demonstrate this strategy by listing the first several pairs on the board: (1, 1), (1, 2), (1, 3), (1, 4), (1, 5), (1, 6), (2, 1), (2, 2), and (2, 3). If students are confused, you may want to list all 36 possible outcomes with them.

The difference between the pair (1, 2) and the pair (2,1) is important, because there are two ways to get a 2 and a 1, but only one way to get two 2s. You can emphasize this point by rolling cubes of two different colors or by marking the faces of one cube with a felt-tip marker or nail polish so it is distinguishable from the other cube.

An efficient way to see all 36 sums is to use a grid with the possible outcomes of one number cube down the side and the possible outcomes of the other number cube along the top. If no one suggests this strategy, bring it up yourself, and work with the class to organize the grid. (Students should keep their finished grids to use for the ACE questions.)

### Cube 2

|        | 1 | 2 | 3 | 4 | 5 | 6 |
|--------|---|---|---|---|---|----|
| 1      | 2 | 3 | 4 | 5 | 6 | 7 |
| 2      | 3 | 4 | 5 | 6 | 7 | 8 |
| 3      | 4 | 5 | 6 | 7 | 8 | 9 |
| 4      | 5 | 6 | 7 | 8 | 9 | 10 |
| 5      | 6 | 7 | 8 | 9 | 10 | 11 |
| 6      | 7 | 8 | 9 | 10 | 11 | 12 |

Cube 1 (rows)

The data can also be represented in a line plot.

```
                        X
                  X     X     X
            X     X     X     X     X
      X     X     X     X     X     X     X
X     X     X     X     X     X     X     X     X
X     X     X     X     X     X     X     X     X     X     X
1     2     3     4     5     6     7     8     9    10    11    12
                              Sum
```

Once the class has created the chart, you may want to ask a few additional questions.

When we roll two number cubes, how many different number pairs are possible? (*36*) Are these pairs equally likely? (*yes*)

How many different sums are possible? (*11*) Are these sums equally likely? (*no*)

When you roll two number cubes, what is the probability that the sum will be 12? ($\frac{1}{36}$) What is the probability that the sum will be 1? (*0*) What is the probability that the sum will be 0? (*0*)

What is the probability that the sum will be a factor of 36? (*2, 3, 4, 6, 9, and 12 are the sums that are factors of 36. These are the sums of 16 of the 36 possible outcomes, so the probability is $\frac{16}{36} = \frac{4}{9}$.*)

What is the probability that the sum will be a prime number? (*The prime sums are 2, 3, 5, 7, and 11. These are sums of 15 of the 36 possible outcomes, so the probability is $\frac{15}{36} = \frac{5}{12}$.*)

Ask students to make up more probability questions that can be answered from the grid.

A good way to wrap up the problem is to play a game of Roller Derby as a class. Divide the class into two teams, and choose one person from each team to be the captain. Post the numbers 1 through 12 on each side of the room. Have the players on each team be the "markers" by arranging themselves in front of the numbers. To start the game, one of the captains rolls a pair of number cubes, and if a teammates' number corresponds to the sum, that person sits down. The first team with all of its members sitting down wins.

# Additional Answers

## Answers to Problem 5.1 Follow-Up

1.  a.

|        |   | **Cube 2** |   |   |   |   |   |
|--------|---|---|---|---|---|----|----|
|        |   | 1 | 2 | 3 | 4 | 5  | 6  |
|        | 1 | 2 | 3 | 4 | 5 | 6  | 7  |
|        | 2 | 3 | 4 | 5 | 6 | 7  | 8  |
|        | 3 | 4 | 5 | 6 | 7 | 8  | 9  |
| **Cube 1** | 4 | 5 | 6 | 7 | 8 | 9  | 10 |
|        | 5 | 6 | 7 | 8 | 9 | 10 | 11 |
|        | 6 | 7 | 8 | 9 | 10| 11 | 12 |

c.  The chart shows how many times each sum occurs in the 36 possible rolls. The sums of 6, 7, and 8 occur most often. The sum of 7 occurs six times, and the sums of 6 and 8 each occur five times.

| Sum | 2 | 3 | 4 | 5 | 6 | 7 | 8 | 9 | 10 | 11 | 12 |
|-----|---|---|---|---|---|---|---|---|----|----|----|
| Number of occurrences | 1 | 2 | 3 | 4 | 5 | 6 | 5 | 4 | 3 | 2 | 1 |

2. There are more ways to get sums that are closer to the middle numbers (6, 7, and 8), so the markers should be clustered toward the middle. Possible distribution:

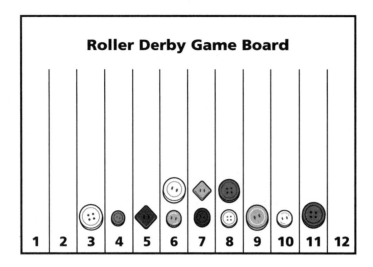

## ACE Answers

### *Connections*

9. yes; There are 18 ways to get an even sum and 18 ways to get an odd sum, so the chances of winning are $\frac{1}{2}$ for both players.

---

**For the Teacher: Fairness of Odds and Evens Game**

Some students may focus on the *number* of even sums and the *number* of odd sums rather than on the number of ways to get an odd or an even sum; that is, there are only 11 sums, 5 odd and 6 even. If you find them making this mistake, discuss the question, emphasizing that there are different ways to get the sums and that the game is fair because there are 18 ways to get an even sum and 18 ways to get an odd sum.

---

**10d.** $\frac{2}{36} + \frac{2}{36} + \frac{2}{36} = \frac{6}{36} = \frac{1}{6}$

**10e.** $\frac{1}{36} + \frac{2}{36} + \frac{2}{36} + \frac{2}{36} + \frac{4}{36} + \frac{2}{36} + \frac{2}{36} + \frac{2}{36} = \frac{17}{36}$

**10f.** $\frac{2}{36} + \frac{2}{36} + \frac{1}{36} + \frac{2}{36} + \frac{1}{36} = \frac{8}{36} = \frac{2}{9}$

**12.** This is a fair game of chance, since there are four equally likely outcomes (HH, HT, TH, and TT) and two of the four outcomes match and two don't match (the probability of winning is $\frac{1}{2}$ for each player).

## For the Teacher: Testing for Fairness

Students might need to find the experimental probabilities to become convinced that the game is fair. They might look at the possibilities as three outcomes—two heads, two tails, and one of each—and realize they are not equally likely because there are two ways to get one head and one tail. This is a good opportunity to challenge them on their use of the formula for theoretical probabilities. Ask the students why the probability of getting two heads is not $\frac{1}{3}$. (Because we cannot use the formula unless the outcomes are equally likely.)

# More About Games of Chance

In this investigation, for the first time, students are asked to devise a simulation to find experimental probabilities. They have experimented with spinners and number cubes before, but this time they are not told what to use.

In Problem 6.1, Scratching Spots, students analyze a toy store's scratch-off card contest. They find the probability of winning a prize first by experimenting with the game and then by analyzing the possible outcomes. To analyze the game, they devise a simulation that may be nothing like scratch-off cards, yet is mathematically the same. The strategy for analyzing theoretical probabilities in this investigation is to list all the possibilities systematically.

## Mathematical and Problem-Solving Goals

- **To gain experience in choosing appropriate simulation strategies**

- **To understand, find, and compare experimental and theoretical probabilities**

- **To gain experience in critically analyzing and interpreting probabilistic statements**

| Materials | | |
|---|---|---|
| Problem | For students | For the teacher |
| 6.1 | Calculators, materials for simulating the contest, such as blocks, spinners, and sheets of card stock for making cards | Transparency 6.1 (optional), scratch-off game card (optional) |

# INVESTIGATION 6

# More About Games of Chance

**H**ave you ever tried to win a contest? Stores and restaurants often have contests to attract customers. Knowing something about probability can often help you figure out your chances of winning these contests.

## 6.1 Scratching Spots

Tawanda's Toys is having a contest! Any customer who spends at least $10 receives a scratch-off game card. Each card has five gold spots that reveal the names of video games when they are scratched. Exactly two spots match on each card. A customer may scratch off only two spots on a card; if the spots match, the customer wins the video game under those spots.

---

**Problem 6.1**

If you play this game once, what is your probability of winning? To answer this question, do the following two things:

**A.** Create a way to simulate Tawanda's contest, and find the experimental probability of winning.

**B.** Analyze the different ways you can scratch off two spots, and find the theoretical probability of winning a prize with one game card.

---

---

## Answers to Problem 6.1

A. Answers will vary. If a large number of trials were conducted, the experimental probability should be close to $\frac{1}{10}$.

B. There are ten equally likely outcomes (pairs of spots). Of these outcomes, only one is the pair of matching spots, so the probability of winning the game is $\frac{1}{10}$.

### At a Glance

***Grouping:***
***Small Groups***

#### Launch

- Introduce the scratch-off game.

- As a class, propose and analyze ways to simulate the game.

#### Explore

- Have each group plan and conduct a simulation and find experimental and theoretical probabilities.

- After they complete the problem, ask the groups to move on to the follow-up.

#### Summarize

- Have the groups report on the simulations they used and the results of their experiments.

- Compare the theoretical and experimental probabilities.

- Discuss the follow-up questions.

### Assignment Choices

ACE questions 1–4 (3 makes an excellent in-class activity, 5–7 are good discussion problems, and 8–11 work well for extra credit or as an extended assignment) and unassigned choices from earlier problems

## Problem 6.1 Follow-Up

**1. a.** If you play Tawanda's scratch-off game 100 times, how many video games would you expect to win?

   **b.** How much money would you have to spend to play the game 100 times?

**2.** Tawanda wants to be sure she will not lose money on her contest. The video games she gives as prizes cost her about $15 each. Will Tawanda lose money on this contest? Why or why not?

**3.** Suppose you play Tawanda's game 20 times and never win. Would you conclude that the game is unfair? For example, would you think that there were not two matching spots on every card? Why or why not?

## Answers to Problem 6.1 Follow-Up

1. a. Since the probability of winning is $\frac{1}{10}$, you could expect to win about once out of every 10 times—so if you play 100 times, you could expect to win about 10 video games.

   b. To play 100 times, you would have to spend at least $1000.

2. Tawanda will probably not lose money. For every ten games customers play, she has sold at least $100 worth of merchandise and can expect to give away one $15 game. (This does not mean Tawanda makes $85 in profit. The merchandise the customers bought cost Tawanda money; we would need to know how much profit she makes from that merchandise to know whether she could lose money on this game.)

**Applications • Connections • Extensions**

As you work on these ACE questions, use your calculator whenever you need it.

# Applications

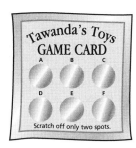

Tawanda's Toys
**GAME CARD**
A       B       C

D       E       F

Scratch off only two spots.

**1.** Tawanda thinks there should be fewer winners in her contest. She has decided to order new cards with six spots. Two of the spots on each card match. What is the probability that a person who plays the game once will win a prize?

**2.** The Kalikak High School Science Club is hosting a carnival to raise money for a trip to the national science fair in San Diego, California. They will have a game called Making Purple at the carnival. The game involves the two spinners below. A player spins spinner A and spinner B. If the player gets red on spinner A and blue on spinner B, the player wins, because red and blue together make purple.

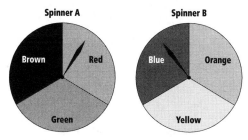

**a.** List the outcomes that are possible when both spinners are spun. Are these outcomes equally likely? Explain your reasoning.

**b.** What is the theoretical probability that a player will "make purple"? Explain.

**c.** If 100 people play this game, how many people would you expect to win? Explain your reasoning.

**d.** The science club will charge $1.00 per spin. A player who makes purple wins $5.00. If 100 people play, how much money would you expect the science club to make?

---

**3.** The game is not necessarily unfair. Just because we expect to win once in ten games, we cannot assume this will always happen. It is possible to play hundreds of times and never win, although it is very unlikely that this would happen.

### Applications

**1.** Fifteen equally likely combinations are possible: AB, AC, AD, AE, AF, BC, BD, BE, BF, CD, CE, CF, DE, DF, and EF. Of these, one is a matching pair, so the probability of winning is $\frac{1}{15}$.

**2a.** There are nine possible outcomes: brown-blue, brown-orange, brown-yellow, red-blue, red-orange, red-yellow, green-blue, green-orange, and green-yellow. These outcomes are equally likely, since each spinner has the same number of spaces and all of the spaces are the same size.

**2b.** $\frac{1}{9}$; Purple (red-blue) is one of the nine equally likely outcomes.

**2c.** About 11 people, since $9 \times 11 = 99$, and for every 9 people you would expect one winner.

**2d.** About $45, because if 100 people play, $100 would be taken in and about $11 \times \$5 = \$55$ would be given away as prizes.

## Connections

**3a.** Answers will vary. It is *possible* to win with every card, but highly unlikely. The question is, could this advertisement give people the impression that they *will* win with every card? Students will probably answer yes. Whatever answer they give, they need to explain their reasoning.

**3b.** Answers will vary.

# Connections

**3.** The Federal Trade Commission is the part of the U.S. government that makes rules for businesses that buy and sell things. The Federal Trade Commission Act states that an advertisement may be found unlawful if it could deceive someone.

The FTC doesn't need to prove that anyone was actually deceived by an advertisement to decide that it is deceptive and unlawful. To decide whether an ad is deceptive, the FTC considers the "general impression" it makes on a "reasonable person." So even if every statement in an ad is true, the ad is deceptive if it gives an overall false impression. (For example, companies cannot show cows in margarine commercials, because it gives the false impression that margarine is a dairy product.)

**a.** Suppose Tawanda placed this advertisement in the newspaper.

## TAWANDA'S TOYS
### is having a HUGE CONTEST!

Every customer receives a scratch-off card
every time they visit the store!
### Every card is a WINNER!

According to the Federal Trade Commission Act, do you think it is legal for Tawanda to say that "every card is a winner"? Explain your answer.

**b.** Design a better advertisement for Tawanda that will make people excited about the contest but will not lead some to think they will win every time they play.

**4.** A sugarless gum company used to have an advertisement that stated:

*Nine out of ten dentists surveyed recommend sugarless
gum for their patients who chew gum.*

Do you think this statement means that 90% of dentists think their patients should chew sugarless gum? Explain your reasoning.

**5.** Suppose you are the coach of the U.S. all-star baseball team. You need to pick someone to pinch hit for the pitcher. You look over the records of your players and narrow your choices to these three:

| Player | At bats | Hits |
|---|---|---|
| George Brett | 9789 | 3005 |
| Kirby Puckett | 5645 | 1812 |
| Wade Boggs | 6213 | 2098 |

Source: Mike Meserole (ed.) *1993 Sports Almanac* (Boston: Houghton Mifflin), p. 109.

**a.** What percent of Brett's at bats were hits? Puckett's? Boggs'?

**b.** Which player has the greatest chance of getting a hit on his next turn at bat? Explain your reasoning.

**4.** Possible answer: no; Most dentists probably do not recommend chewing gum at all, but of those surveyed, most feel that if their patients are going to chew gum anyway, it should be sugarless.

**5a.** Brett: 30.9%; Puckett: 32.1%; Boggs: 33.8%

**5b.** Answers will vary. Students who base their answers solely on the percents will choose Boggs (this is like looking at experimental probabilities, only we didn't gather the data ourselves). Students may have good reasons for other answers (for example, Brett has more experience pinch-hitting). Don't ignore real-life concerns that may appear nonmathematical; students need to use mathematics sensibly, along with their knowledge about other aspects of their lives, to make good decisions.

**6a.** neither; Individual passengers do not affect an airplane's ability to fly or its chances of crashing.

**6b.** yes; If they are on the same plane, neither has a greater chance of being in an accident than the other. (**Teaching Tip:** With question 6, we want to combat students' notions that someone's "luck can run out." If students think that one airplane passenger in **6a** can be more likely than another to get in an accident, this question might help them see that both passengers are in the same plane and would have the same experience on this flight.)

**7a.** no; The graph starts at 95%, so the bars are not proportional in that way.

**7b.** Answers will vary. There are many relevant things we don't know. For example, we don't know how many trucks of each brand were considered, or if each company has been making trucks for 10 years. This last issue is important because if company A has manufactured most of its vehicles during the most recent 5 years, we would expect a higher percentage of company A's trucks to still be on the road.

### Extensions

**8.** Answers will vary.

---

**6.** Willie Mae has flown over a million miles as an airline passenger without ever being in an accident. Kobie has never flown in an airplane. Both are planning to take a trip in an airplane.

   **a.** Who do you think is more likely to be in an airplane accident? Why?

   **b.** Does your answer to part a make sense if Willie Mae and Kobie get on the same airplane? Explain.

**7.** A-1 Trucks used this graph to show that their trucks last longer than other companies' trucks. A-1 Trucks is company A on the graph.

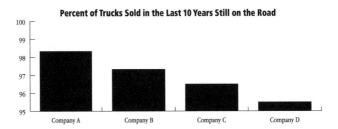

**Percent of Trucks Sold in the Last 10 Years Still on the Road**

   **a.** The bar for company A is about six times as tall as the bar for company D. Does this mean that the chances of one of company A's trucks lasting 10 years are about six times as great as the chances of one of company D's trucks lasting 10 years? Explain your reasoning.

   **b.** If you wanted to buy a truck, would this graph convince you to buy a truck from company A? Why or why not?

## Extensions

**8.** Refer to the discussion of the Federal Trade Commission Act in question 3 above. Find an advertisement that might be deceptive, and bring it in to discuss with your class. You might consider contacting the company, telling them why you think the ad might be deceptive, and asking for proof of their claims. The company is required by law to respond.

In 9–11, imagine that you help businesses by designing promotional contests. Design a contest for each company. Each contest should help the company attract customers, but not make the company lose money. For each contest, explain the rules, including any requirements for entering the contest, and design an advertisement for the contest.

**9.** The Fashion Gallery is a small clothing store. Its manager would like you to design a contest in which 1 of every 30 players wins a prize.

**10.** Supermart Superstores is a chain of supermarkets with over 100 locations. The director of operations would like to have a contest with a $100,000 grand prize!

**11.** Ally's AutoWorld sells new and used cars. Ally would like to have a contest with lots of winners and fairly big prizes. She would like about one out of every ten players to win a $500 prize.

**Investigation 6: More About Games of Chance** 55

**ACE**

9. Answers will vary.
10. Answers will vary.
11. Answers will vary.

## Possible Answers

**1.** You would first establish the probabilities, either by experimentation or by analyzing the situation and listing all possible outcomes. If the five spots are A, B, C, D, and E, there are ten equally likely ways to scratch off two of the five spots: AB, AC, AD, AE, BC, BD, BE, CD, CE, and DE. Since one of these ten combinations is the matching pair, the probability of winning is $\frac{1}{10}$. In 1000 games, we would expect to win about $\frac{1}{10} \times 1000 =$ 100 times.

**2.** For a six-spot game, 15 equally likely combinations are possible: AB, AC, AD, AE, AF, BC, BD, BE, BF, CD, CE, CF, DE, DF, and EF. One of these is a matching pair, so the probability of winning is $\frac{1}{15}$. In 1000 games, you would expect to win about $\frac{1}{15} \times 1000 =$ 67 times.

**3.** To determine whether it is a fair game of chance, you would have to figure how much it will cost you to play a certain number of games and what you would expect to win. Since the probability of winning is $\frac{1}{6}$, you can think about playing 12 times to give you an idea about what to expect. In 12 games, you would expect to win about 2 times, which means you would win about $1.00. However, it would cost you $1.20 to play 12 games. Since your winnings are less than the cost to play, this is not a fair game of chance.

# Mathematical Reflections

**I**n this investigation, you examined what you might *expect* to gain or lose when you play a game of chance. These questions will help you summarize what you have learned:

1. How can you find the number of times you would expect to win if you play Tawanda's game on a five-spot card 1000 times?

2. How can you find the number of times you would expect to win if you play Tawanda's game on a six-spot card 1000 times?

3. Suppose that your probability of winning a game at the school fair is $\frac{1}{6}$. It costs 10¢ to play the game, and the prize for winning is 50¢. Describe how you could decide whether this is a fair game of chance. (A *fair game of chance* is one in which you would expect to break even in the long run.)

Think about your answers to these questions, discuss your ideas with other students and your teacher, and then write a summary of your findings in your journal.

 **How Likely Is It?**

## Tips for the Linguistically Diverse Classroom

**Original Rebus** The Original Rebus technique is described in detail in *Getting to Know Connected Mathematics*. Students make a copy of the text before it is discussed. During discussion, they generate their own rebuses for words they do not understand as the words are made comprehensible through pictures, objects, or demonstrations. Example: Question 2—key words for which students may make rebuses are *number* (#), *win* (a jackpot with an explanation point), *six-spot card* (a card with six spots).

# TEACHING THE INVESTIGATION

## 6.1 • Scratching Spots

Many Americans find themselves on the losing end of games of chance. Frequently the advertising for such games is misleading at best. This problem gives students an opportunity to simulate and analyze a popular game of chance. If you happen to have a scratch-off game card, it makes a nice addition to the lesson, especially for students who have never seen one.

### Launch

Read the introductory text and the problem with students, and discuss possible ways of finding the experimental probability of winning a prize with one game card. This will involve doing a *simulation*. Students will need to devise a simulation that is mathematically equivalent to scratching off two spots on a five-spot game card.

One way to simulate the game is to put two red blocks, one white block, one yellow block, and one blue block in an opaque container, then draw two blocks at a time. Drawing the two red blocks is equivalent to scratching off the two matching spots. Another possibility is to have five students act as the "spots" in the front of the room, holding cards that are hidden from the rest of the class. Two students hold cards with matching symbols, and three hold cards with three other symbols. Another student chooses two of the five students to reveal their cards. After each guess, students mix up their cards.

Students may have other ideas for simulating the contest. Analyze their suggestions with them: there should be exactly one matching pair among five choices. If students suggest using spinners, help them to see that in order to simulate the game, the result they get on the first spin can no longer be available on the second spin; they could use a five-part spinner for the first spin and a four-part spinner for the second spin. The labels on the four-part spinner would have to be adjusted according to what happened on the first spin.

### Explore

Students must decide for themselves how to collect the data and when they have collected enough data to find a reasonable experimental probability. The groups may use different simulation methods. Encourage students to use any method that makes sense to them as long as it is mathematically equivalent to the scratch-off game.

Allow the groups to plan and carry out their simulations, collect their data, and find the experimental probability. When they have completed their experiment, students should move on to part B in which they analyze the outcomes and compute the theoretical probabilities.

After they complete the problem, ask the groups to work on the follow-up questions.

## Summarize

Have the groups share their solutions and strategies with the class. Discuss the different methods of simulating the game.

To analyze the situation and find the theoretical probability, most students will make an organized list to figure out how many ways there are to choose two spots. Here is one way to make the list; the spots are labeled A, B, C, D, and E to help make listing easier.

| AB | AC | AD | AE |
|----|----|----|----|
|    | BC | BD | BE |
|    |    | CD | CE |
|    |    |    | DE |

This list shows that there are ten ways to scratch off the spots. One of these ten combinations is the matching pair, so the probability of winning is $\frac{1}{10}$. Notice that the order in which the spots in a pair are chosen does not matter; the card will look the same no matter which spot is scratched off first. If students want to list each pair twice with the letters reversed, there would be 20 pairs—2 of which would be winners—which also gives a probability of $\frac{2}{20}$ or $\frac{1}{10}$.

After you have summarized the problem, discuss the follow-up questions. To continue the discussion, you may wish to do ACE question 3 as a class activity.

# Probability and Genetics

**T**his investigation introduces biology as a source of applications for probability.

In Problem 7.1, Curling Your Tongue, students determine how many of the students in the class can curl their tongues and use this data to make predictions about the probability of any one student being able to curl his or her tongue. In Problem 7.2, Tracing Traits, this experimental method is compared with the way in which geneticists study a person's traits: by examining the genetic makeup of the person's parents, grandparents, and other relatives. Students then gain experience with determining whether people have the tongue-curling trait based on the genetic probabilities. In the ACE questions, students apply what they have learned about genetics and probability to determine probabilities associated with eye color.

## Mathematical and Problem-Solving Goals

- **To increase understanding of experimental and theoretical probability**

- **To appreciate the power of probability for making predictions and decisions**

| Materials | | |
|---|---|---|
| **Problem** | **For students** | **For the teacher** |
| **All** | Calculators | Transparencies 7.1 and 7.2 (optional) |

Student Pages 57–64    Teaching the Investigation 64a–64d

# INVESTIGATION 7

# Probability and Genetics

**H**ave you ever wondered why your eyes and your hair are the color they are? Scientists who study traits such as eye and hair color are called *geneticists*. Geneticists use probabilities to predict the occurrence of certain traits in children based on the traits of their parents, grandparents, and other relatives.

One interesting genetic trait is the ability to curl the tongue into a U shape. In this investigation you will explore the question, What are the chances that someone can curl his or her tongue?

## 7.1 Curling Your Tongue

One day Kalvin was teasing his little sister Kyla, and he stuck his tongue out at her. She noticed that his tongue was curled into a U shape. Kyla said, "That's weird, Kalvin—your tongue looks goofy!"

Kalvin looked in the mirror and noticed that he *could* curl his tongue. He wondered how many other people can curl their tongues.

> ### Problem 7.1
>
> What fraction of students in your class can curl their tongues?
> With your class, conduct a survey of the students in the class to investigate tongue curling and to answer this question.

**Investigation 7: Probability and Genetics** 57

### Launch

- Discuss the genetic trait of tongue curling.

- As a class, collect data on whether each student in class has the tongue-curling trait.

### Explore

- Have students work in pairs on the follow-up also.

### Summarize

- As a class, discuss the answers to the follow-up question.

## Answer to Problem 7.1

Answers will vary.

## Assignment Choices

ACE questions 7, 8a and 8b, and unassigned choices from earlier problems

# Tracing Traits

### Launch

- Discuss geneticists and the study of inherited traits.

- Have students read the background information about genetics, or present it in a class discussion.

### Explore

- Have pairs or groups of three investigate the problem.

- Encourage students to make charts to display the possible allele combinations.

### Summarize

- As a class, review the charts and what they reveal.

- Discuss the follow-up questions.

## Assignment Choices

ACE questions 1–6, 9, and unassigned choices from earlier problems

## Assessment

It is appropriate to use Check-Up 2 after this problem.

■ **Problem 7.1 Follow-Up**

What is the probability that a student you choose randomly from the hallway of your school will be able to curl his or her tongue?

### 7.2 Tracing Traits

Surveys are often used to gather information about a group of people, or a *population*. For example, if scientists want to find out the percent of people in a population that have a certain disease, they might conduct a survey of a large number of people. Sometimes scientists are interested in the probability that a *specific person* has a certain trait or will have a particular disease. In these situations, geneticists study the traits of the person's parents, grandparents, and other family members.

Have you ever heard of *genes?* (We don't mean the kind you wear!) Your parents gave you a unique set of genes that determines many of your traits, such as your eye color, whether you are color blind, whether you will be bald someday, and whether you can curl your tongue.

### Did you know?

**P**sychologists have long been interested in investigating how great a part genes play in determining human intelligence. One way of learning more about this topic is by studying identical twins who have been separated at a young age and raised in very different kinds of homes. Studies have shown that such twins showed remarkable similarities in intelligence. One study showed that twins raised in different home environments had IQ scores almost as close as those of identical twins raised in the same home. Since identical twins have the exact same set of genes, these results support the idea that genes play a key role in human intelligence.

Even more surprising was learning that these twins also were very similar in physical appearance, dress, mannerisms, preferences, attitudes, and even personality. Many of the twins had similar hairstyles, moved their hands in similar ways, or had the same attitude toward their jobs.

## Answer to Problem 7.1 Follow-Up

Answers will vary. The class can use the experimental probability found for the tongue-curling trait in the class to estimate the probability for the entire school population.

Geneticists use the word *allele* to mean a special form of a gene. For example, you have two alleles that determine whether or not you can curl your tongue. Each of your parents also has two alleles for tongue curling. You received one of your alleles from your mother and one from your father. Each of your mother's two alleles had an equal chance of being passed on to you, and each of your father's two alleles had an equal chance of being passed on to you.

Let's let a capital T stand for the allele for tongue curling, and a small t stand for the allele for non-tongue curling. If a person receives a T allele from each parent, his tongue-curling alleles will be TT, and he will be able to curl his tongue. If a person receives a t allele from each parent, his tongue-curling alleles will be tt, and he won't be able to curl his tongue. What if a person receives one T allele and one t allele? Nature has figured out a way to break this tie. In the case of tongue curling, the T allele is *dominant,* and the t allele is *recessive.* This means that if a person has a Tt allele combination, the T allele dominates, and the person has the tongue-curling trait.

If your tongue-curling alleles are TT or Tt, you can curl your tongue. If your tongue-curling alleles are tt, you won't be able to curl your tongue—no matter how hard you try!

### An Example: Bonnie and Ebert's Baby

Bonnie and Ebert are going to have a baby. Bonnie's tongue-curling alleles are Tt, and Ebert's tongue-curling alleles are tt. You can determine the probability that their baby will be able to curl his or her tongue. Here is a diagram of the allele possibilities for the baby:

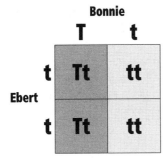

Ebert's alleles are shown at the left side, and Bonnie's alleles are shown at the top. The Tt in the upper-left square is the combination of Bonnie's T allele and Ebert's t allele.

### Answer to Problem 7.2

The possibilities for Kalvin's new sibling's alleles can be shown in a chart.

The possibilities for the child are TT, Tt, Tt, and tt. Since three out of four of these equally likely possibilities include the dominant tongue-curling allele (T), the probability that the baby will inherit the trait is $\frac{3}{4}$.

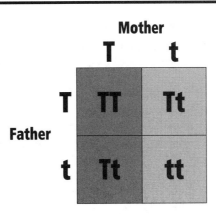

You can see that there are four possible allele pairs (outcomes). Two of these pairs—Tt and Tt—result in the tongue-curling trait. So, the probability that Bonnie and Ebert's baby will have the tongue-curling trait is $\frac{2}{4}$ or $\frac{1}{2}$.

The probability of a child being able to curl his or her tongue will not always be $\frac{1}{2}$. If the parents' alleles are different from Ebert and Bonnie's, the probability will be different.

### Problem 7.2

Kalvin's mother is pregnant with her third child. Kalvin figured out from studying his family for several generations that his mother and father both have the tongue-curling alleles Tt. Based on what you know about his parent's alleles, what is the probability that Kalvin's new sibling will be able to curl his or her tongue?

### ■ Problem 7.2 Follow-Up

**1.** Neither of Eileen's parents can curl their tongues. What is the probability that Eileen can curl her tongue?

**2.** Suppose that Geoff's tongue-curling alleles are TT and Mali's tongue-curling alleles are Tt. What is the probability that their child will be able to curl his or her tongue?

**3.** Marc can curl his tongue, and he wonders whether his parents can. He asks his mother to try it, and she can't curl hers. Do you think Marc's father can curl his tongue? Why or why not?

**4.** If Rodney's mother and father can both curl their tongues, can you conclude that Rodney can curl his tongue? Explain.

There are many other dominant traits that you can study in the way you have just studied tongue curling. For example, brown eyes are dominant over blue eyes, having a hairy head as an adult is dominant over having a bald head as an adult, and having a "hitchhiker's thumb" (also called a double-jointed thumb) is dominant over not having it.

## Answers to Problem 7.2 Follow-Up

1. Eileen's parents' alleles must be tt and tt (if either had a T, then he or she would have the trait). Eileen's alleles must therefore be tt, and the probability that she can curl her tongue is 0.

2. The four possibilities for Geoff and Mali's child are TT, TT, Tt, and Tt. The child's alleles must contain at least one T, so the probability that the child will be able to curl his or her tongue is 1.

3. Since Marc can curl his tongue, he must have the alleles TT or Tt. Since his mother cannot curl her tongue, her alleles must be tt. Marc's father must therefore have at least one T allele and he can curl his tongue.

4. no; Rodney's father and mother may both have Tt, and Rodney could therefore have inherited tt and not have the trait.

**Applications • Connections • Extensions**

As you work on these ACE questions, use your calculator whenever you need it.

# Applications

In 1–6, use the following information about the genetics of eye color to answer the question. The alleles for blue eyes and brown eyes work similarly to tongue-curling alleles. Let B stand for the brown-eyes allele, and let b stand for the blue-eyes allele. B is dominant, so a person with BB or Bb will have brown eyes, while a person with bb will have blue eyes. (You may have noticed that we have not talked about green eyes and other variations. These things can get pretty complicated—you might learn more about this in your high-school science classes.)

**1.** Suppose two blue-eyed people are expecting a baby. What is the probability that their child will have brown eyes? Explain.

**2.** Suppose a brown-eyed person with alleles BB and a blue-eyed person are expecting a baby. What is the probability that the baby will have brown eyes? Explain.

**3.** If Laura has brown eyes, could both of her parents have blue eyes? Why or why not?

**4.** If Katrina has blue eyes, could both of her parents have brown eyes? Why or why not?

**5.** Suppose Ken and Andrea both have brown eyes. They are wondering how many of their children will have brown eyes.

    **a.** Andrea's mother has brown eyes, and her father has blue eyes. What are Andrea's eye-color alleles? Explain.

    **b.** Ken's mother has blue eyes, and his father has brown eyes. What are Ken's eye-color alleles? Explain.

    **c.** What is the probability that Ken and Andrea's first child will have brown eyes?

    **d.** If their first child has brown eyes, what is the probability that their second child will also have brown eyes?

    **e.** Suppose Ken and Andrea have ten children. How many of their children would you expect to have brown eyes? Why?

## Answers

### Applications

**1.** 0; The blue-eyed parents must both have bb, and therefore the child will have bb.

**2.** 1; When BB is paired with bb, the only possibility for the baby is Bb.

**3.** no; If both of her parents have bb, Laura would have to have bb too.

**4.** yes; Her parents could both have Bb, giving their children a $\frac{1}{4}$ chance of inheriting bb and having blue eyes.

**5a.** Andrea must have Bb—B because she has brown eyes, and b because she must have inherited a b from her father, who has bb.

**5b.** Ken must also have Bb, for the same reason Andrea does.

**5c.** The possibilities for the child's eye-color alleles are BB, Bb, Bb, and bb. The probability that the child will inherit brown eyes (BB, Bb, or Bb) is $\frac{3}{4}$.

**5d.** $\frac{3}{4}$; The first child's eye color has no effect on the eye color of the second child.

**5e.** If they have ten children, we expect that seven or eight of them will have brown eyes, because $\frac{3}{4}$ of 10 is 7.5.

**6a.** Dawn has blue eyes and therefore has bb.

**6b.** Tomas must have a B since he has brown eyes. Since his son has blue eyes, he must also have a b. Tomas's alleles are therefore Bb.

**6c.** The possibilities for the baby are Bb, bb, Bb, and bb. Hence, the probability that the baby will have blue eyes is $\frac{1}{2}$.

### Connections

**7.** Possible answer: *Probability* is the chance that something will occur, or an estimate of the fraction of times that something will occur over the long run.

**8a.** Possible answer: Experimental probabilities are based on experiments, while theoretical probabilities are found by analyzing possible outcomes. An experimental probability becomes closer to the theoretical probability when it is based on more and more trials.

**8b.** We were finding an experimental probability, because we were carrying out an experiment— a survey—to determine the probability.

**8c.** We were finding a theoretical probability, because we listed all the possible outcomes to determine the probability.

**6.** Suppose you are a geneticist and you are trying to determine Dawn and Tomas's eye-color alleles. Here is the information you have:

• Dawn has blue eyes.

• Tomas has brown eyes.

• Their two daughters have brown eyes.

• Their son has blue eyes.

**a.** What are Dawn's eye-color alleles?

**b.** What are Tomas's eye-color alleles?

**c.** If they have another child, what is the probability that he or she will have blue eyes?

## Connections

**7.** Write your own definition for the word *probability*. In your definition, show what you have learned about probability during this unit.

**8. a.** Write your own explanation about how experimental and theoretical probabilities are alike and different.

**b.** When you surveyed your classmates to find the probability that a student has the tongue-curling trait, were you finding an experimental or a theoretical probability? Explain.

**c.** When you found the probability that Kalvin's new sibling would have the tongue-curling trait, were you finding an experimental or theoretical probability? Explain.

# Extensions

**9.** Pick one of the following two options:

**a.** Investigate tongue curling in your family. Make a family tree that shows the tongue-curling alleles that you can figure out for each person. Trace back as many generations as you can. (If you'd like, you may do this for eye color instead.)

**b.** Survey a large number of people to estimate the percent of people in the population who can curl their tongues. Represent the data in a graph. How do these data compare with your class's data?

**9.** Answers will vary. Two options are offered for this extension because of the difficulty that some students—for example, those who are adopted or who live with one or neither parent—will have in making a family allele tree.

**1.** We used relative frequencies from our class survey to estimate the probability that a student in the general population would be able to curl his or her tongue.

**2.** In the theoretical analysis, we were using information on how tongue curling is passed from one generation to another through alleles. This allowed us to reason about parents from information about children and to reason about the chances of a child being able to curl his or her tongue by looking at the possible combinations of the parents' alleles. This was using probability to predict the chances that a child would inherit the trait (this depends on knowing the parents' alleles).

**3.** Since tongue curling is dominant, if a child inherits a tongue-curling allele from one parent, the child will be able to curl his or her tongue. If both parents can curl their tongues, then each parent has either TT or Tt. If one parent has TT, then no matter what the other parent has, the child will inherit a T allele and the tongue-curling trait. If both parents have Tt, the child has a $\frac{1}{4}$ chance of inheriting tt and not having the trait; each parent has passed a recessive gene to the child. Therefore, tongue-curling parents can have children who don't carry the trait.

# Mathematical Reflections

**I**n this investigation, you studied an example of a way that probabilities are used to predict a person's characteristics, such as eye color or tongue curling. These questions will help you summarize what you have learned:

**1** How was probability used in your class's tongue-curling experiment?

**2** How was probability used in your theoretical analysis of tongue curling?

**3** If both parents of a child can curl their tongues, will the child be able to curl his or her tongue? Explain.

Think about your answers to these questions, discuss your ideas with other students and your teacher, and then write a summary of your findings in your journal.

## Tips for the Linguistically Diverse Classroom

**Diagram Code** The Diagram Code technique is described in detail in *Getting to Know Connected Mathematics*. Students use a minimal number of words and drawings, diagrams, or symbols to respond to questions that require writing. Example: Question 3—A student might answer this question by drawing three sets of stick figures, each of which shows two parents and a child. In the first set, the parents would each be labeled *TT*, and the child would be labled *yes*. In the second set, the parents would be labeled *TT* and *Tt*, and the child would be labeled *yes*. In the third set, the parents would be labeled *Tt* and *Tt* and the child would be labeled $\frac{1}{4}$ *chance no*, $\frac{3}{4}$ *chance yes*.

# TEACHING THE INVESTIGATION

## 7.1 • Curling Your Tongue

This whole-class activity is designed to investigate the distribution of the tongue-curling trait (the ability to roll up the edges of the tongue to make a trough in the middle) in the students' school population. You may want a few students to demonstrate tongue curling.

### Launch

As a class, conduct a survey to determine how many students in class can curl their tongues; the class may need to vote on how to count students whose tongue-curling trait seems borderline. Record the data on the board.

---

**For the Teacher: Tongue Curling**

When students are talking about tongue curling, try to persuade them not to attach a value to having or not having the trait. You might point out that tongue curling is a genetic characteristic like eye color and makes no difference to the quality of one's life; it's just interesting to explore the distribution of the trait.

---

### Explore

After the class has conducted its survey, have students investigate the follow-up question in pairs.

### Summarize

As a class, discuss the follow-up question. Ask students if they feel confident in their predictions about the probability that a randomly selected student can curl his or her tongue.

We do not intend for students to actually survey other students outside of class, but to realize that their classroom data serves as an estimate of the distribution of the trait in the larger school population. Students may see that a larger sample would be more predictive and want to collect additional data.

## 7.2 • Tracing Traits

Students have just found the experimental probability of someone in the school being able to curl his or her tongue. We are not moving on to finding theoretical probabilities for tongue curling, because an analysis of the distribution of the trait is fairly difficult. Instead, we will examine theoretical probabilities of *specific* people being able to curl their tongues based on the genetic makeup of their families. Check with the science teacher about whether your students have studied any genetics and for possible assistance with the analysis or extensions.

## Launch

To help students make the transition to Problem 7.2, which is a minilesson in genetics, discuss what a geneticist is and does. Geneticists may sample a population to determine the frequency of traits such as tongue curling. They also may study people's genes to determine which traits they have. Thousands of traits are genetically inherited, such as hair color, eye color, curly versus straight hair, hitchhiker's (double-jointed) thumb, and attached versus detached ear lobes. Bring up tongue curling as another example of an inherited trait.

The student edition presents a summary of the genetics information students need to know. Have students read the genetics information in the student edition, or study the information yourself and present it to them. They may already be familiar with the term *gene*. An *allele* is a certain form of a gene and is the more correct term to use when discussing the different forms of a gene, such as dominant and recessive. Students—and teachers—should not feel distressed if they are not confident in their knowledge of genetics. You may want to recommend further reading for students who are especially interested in this topic, and you or your students can ask the science teacher more about genetics.

As you talk about the example of Ebert and Bonnie, emphasize that the four possibilities are equally likely, and therefore we can conclude that the probability of the baby inheriting the tongue-curling trait is $\frac{2}{4}$ or $\frac{1}{2}$, and of not inheriting it is also $\frac{1}{2}$.

Discuss the story in Problem 7.2. Students may wonder how Kalvin could figure out what his parents' alleles were. If his sister Kyla cannot curl her tongue, but both of their parents can, then Kyla must have tt, meaning that each parent has at least one t. Since both parents can curl their tongues, each must also have a T, giving them both Tt.

## Explore

Have students work in pairs or groups of three to investigate the probability that Kalvin's new sibling will be able to curl her or his tongue. Encourage groups to make a chart, as was done in the example about Bonnie and Ebert, to help them list the possibilities.

---

### For the Teacher: Dominant Traits

Contrary to popular belief, the fact that a trait is dominant does not mean that most of the population has the trait. For example, having an extra finger is a dominant trait, but it is very rare.

A mathematician named G. H. Hardy was the first to note that the proportion of the population with a dominant trait can be very small and still remain fairly constant. This is because a trait being dominant does not mean that it spreads. It only means that when an allele that represents this trait is paired with another allele, the dominant trait will show up.

The dominant alleles will not wipe out the recessive alleles. There may only be a small number of the dominant alleles in the population, so the trait will not spread to a greater percentage of the population. And an allele being dominant does not mean it is more likely to be passed on to children than a recessive allele.

---

## Summarize

Review the groups' charts. Make sure students understand how to analyze the possibilities: any combination containing the dominant allele T means the child will be able to curl his or her tongue. There is only a $\frac{1}{4}$ probability that the child will inherit the tt combination and not have the tongue-curling trait. In the general population, not having the trait is more unique than having it.

Work on the follow-up questions as a class to assess students' understanding of the genetics and mathematics involved.

## Answers

### Using Your Probability Reasoning

**1a.** Using these data, the experimental probability of winning is $\frac{12}{30} = \frac{2}{5} = 40\%$.

**b.** The theoretical probability of winning the game is $\frac{4}{12} = \frac{1}{3} = 33\frac{1}{3}\%$. This can be found by making an organized list of possible outcomes or by utilizing a counting tree.

See p. 64g for a sample organized list and counting tree.

**c.** With a small number of trials, the experimental probability is not always precise. For instance, had we played the game 100 times, we would expect the probability of winning to be closer to the theoretical probability.

## Unit Reflections

**W**orking on problems in this unit, you explored some of the big ideas in *probability*. You learned how to think about *chance* in activities for which individual trials have uncertain outcomes but patterns of outcomes emerge after many trials. You learned how to use *experimental* and *theoretical probabilities* to predict outcomes when tossing number cubes or flipping coins. You found that some events are *equally likely* while other events are not. Most important of all, you learned what makes outcomes of some activities uncertain and how to use mathematics to describe the probabilities of those outcomes.

**Using Your Probability Reasoning**—To test your understanding and skill in the use of probability ideas and techniques, consider examples of how probability is involved in designing and playing carnival games.

**1** *Joanna designed a game for the school carnival. She prepared two bags of marbles.*

*Bag A contains 3 marbles:*
*one red, one blue, and one green.*

*Bag B contains 4 marbles:*
*two reds and two blues.*

*To play the game, a contestant picks one marble from each bag. If the colors of the marbles match, the contestant wins a prize.*

**a.** These are the win/loss results for the first 30 games.

W L L W W L L W W L L W W L L
L W L L L L W L W L W L L L L W W

What do these data suggest about the experimental probability of winning the game?

**b.** What is the theoretical probability of winning the game?

**c.** What explains the difference between your answers to part a and part b?

## How to Use
## *Looking Back and Looking Ahead: Unit Reflections*

The first part of this section includes problems that allow students to demonstrate their mathematical understandings and skills. The second part gives them an opportunity to explain their reasoning. This section can be used as a review to help students stand back and reflect on the "big" ideas and connections in the unit. This section may be assigned as homework, followed up with class discussion the next day. Focus on the *Explaining Your Reasoning* section in the discussion. Encourage the students to refer to the problems to illustrate their reasoning.

**2** *David designed a different game for the carnival. His game uses the spinner pictured at the right. If the spinner lands on a GOLD section, then the player gets a prize.*

   **a.** Does the player have a better chance of winning the bag game or the spinner game?

   **b.** Is it more likely that the spinner will land on GOLD in 2 of the first 3 trials or that the spinner will land on GOLD in 20 of the first 30 trials?

**3** *David also created the five spinners shown below for the carnival. The spinners are shown below. He used one of the spinners 100 times and recorded the results.*

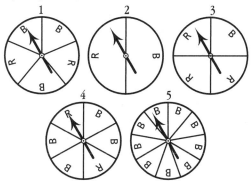

   **a.** Which spinner is most likely the one he used?

   **b.** On which spinner(s) do you have the same chance of getting red or blue?

| Outcome | Blue | Red |
|---------|------|-----|
| Frequency | 28 | 72 |

**Explaining Your Reasoning**—When you use mathematical calculations or diagrams to solve a problem or make a decision, it is important to justify your reasoning. Answer these questions about your work on Problems 1–3.

**1.** When studying activities with uncertain outcomes like games of chance or genetic inheritance,

   **a.** how do you calculate experimental probabilities for the possible outcomes?

   **b.** how do you calculate theoretical probabilities for the possible outcomes?

---

**2a.** Since the theoretical probability of winning the spinner game is also $\frac{1}{3}$ or $33\frac{1}{3}$%, David has an equally likely chance of winning either the bag game or the spinner game.

   **b.** It is more likely that the spinner would land on GOLD in 2 out of the first 3 trials because, as the number of trials increases, the experimental probability approaches the theoretical probability of $\frac{1}{3}$ (or $\frac{10}{30}$). Having 20 GOLD out of 30 spins is less likely.

**3a.** Spinner 3

   **b.** Spinner 2

**Explaining Your Reasoning**
See page 64g.

2. What relationship would you expect between experimental and theoretical probabilities for an uncertain event in a case where the experimental probability is based on

   a. 5 trials?

   b. 50 trials?

   c. 500 trials?

3. Suppose that three friends play a game in which a nickel and a dime are tossed. If neither coin shows heads up, Aisha wins; if two coins show heads up, Billie wins; if one coin shows heads up, Caitlin wins. Caitlin says that this is a fair game because each player has a chance to win.

   a. How would you convince her otherwise?

   b. What would you say to Caitlin if each player has one win in the first three plays and she says, "See, the game is fair"?

4. If you were asked to give five examples of situations in which probability can be used to predict outcomes of uncertain events, what examples would you choose?

The ideas of probability will be used and developed further in several other units of *Connected Mathematics*, especially *Bits and Pieces II* and *What Do You Expect?* You will also find that you can apply probability ideas and reasoning in science and in questions about personal health care, safety, and games of chance.

# Looking Back and Looking Ahead

## Answers

### Using Your Probability Reasoning

**1b.** Organized List

| Bag A | Bag B | Win? |
|---|---|---|
| **R** | **R** | **Yes** |
| **R** | **R** | **Yes** |
| R | B | |
| R | B | |
| B | R | |
| B | R | |
| **B** | **B** | **Yes** |
| **B** | **B** | **Yes** |
| G | R | |
| G | R | |
| G | B | |
| G | B | |

**Counting Tree**   **Win?**

### Explaining Your Reasoning

**1a.** To determine experimental probabilities, several trials of the experiment must be completed so that the results can be used to compute the fraction each outcome occurred out of the total number of trials.

**b.** To determine theoretical probabilities, first make a list of all possible equally likely outcomes by making an organized list or by using a counting tree. Then, for each unique outcome, write a fraction whose numerator is the number of ways this outcome could possibly occur and whose denominator is the total number of possible outcomes. The sum of all of the theoretical probabilities (fractions) is one.

**2.** As the number of trials increases, the closer the experimental probability and the theoretical probability are expected to be.

**3a.** Make a list of all possible outcomes and find the theoretical probabilities. This would show that HH ($\frac{1}{4}$) or TT ($\frac{1}{4}$) can occur only once while HT or TH can occur twice ($\frac{1}{2}$).

**b.** Tell her that we need to play more rounds to see the patterns that emerge over the long run.

**4.** Student responses will vary. Some ideas include: winning a lottery; winning a carnival game of chance; being selected at random to answer a question in class; getting the right answer by guessing on a multiple choice exam; guessing the number of red M&Ms in a bag of 100; predicting how many classmates will grow to be over 6 feet tall.

# Assessment Resources

For the Quiz, each pair will need two chips marked with Xs and Ys as described in the quiz (bingo chips work nicely for this and can be written on with a permanent marker) and a small cup (shaking the chips in a cup instead of flipping them has proved easier for teachers to manage). Additionally, you will need to discuss with your students how each pair's results will be collected on a master chart that you create on the board so that pairs can analyze the entire class's data.

For the Unit Test, each student will need three chips marked with Xs, Ys, and Zs as described on the Unit Test, page 74, and a small cup. Again, students will be combining their data on a class chart and analyzing the entire class's data.

Name _____ Date _____

1. Use this circle to draw a spinner with six sections. Make the spinner so that it is equally likely that the spinner will land in each of the six sections. What fraction of the circle is each section?

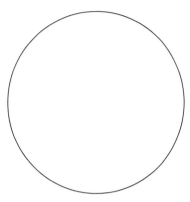

2. Use this circle to draw another spinner with six sections, but make this spinner so that it is *not* equally likely that the spinner will land in each of the six sections. What fraction of the circle is each section?

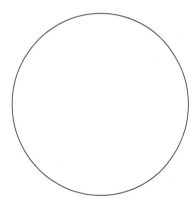

3. a. Give an example of an event that has a 100% chance of happening.

   b. Give an example of an event that is impossible.

## Check-Up 1

    **c.** If an event is impossible, what are the chances that it will occur?

**4.** Rachel has tossed a fair coin ten times, and it has landed heads up every time.

    **a.** Is this possible? Explain.

    **b.** Is this likely? Explain.

    **c.** Which of the following statements is true about what will happen when Rachel tosses the coin again? Why?

        **i.** The coin will land heads up.

        **ii.** The coin will land tails up.

        **iii.** The chances of the coin landing heads up or tails up are equal.

        **iv.** The coin is more likely to land heads up.

        **v.** The coin is more likely to land tails up.

**5.** Two coins are flipped. Alan gets a point if the coins match, and Sondra gets a point if the coins do not match. Which of the following statements is true?

    **a.** Alan is more likely to win.

    **b.** Sondra is more likely to win.

    **c.** Alan and Sondra have the same chances of winning.

    **d.** There is not enough information to decide the chances of either player winning.

    **e.** Sondra can never win.

Explain your answer.

# Quiz

Your class has been asked by a game company to test their newest game, Flip 2 Chips. You and your classmates will be playing and analyzing the game. The company wants to know whether Flip 2 Chips is fair for all players.

---

**Description of Flip 2 Chips**

*Materials:*   Two chips
- One chip has an **X** on both sides.
- One chip has an **X** on one side and a **Y** on the other side.

Small cup

*Rules:*   **1.** Shake the chips in the cup and then pour them out.
**2.** Award points according to what shows on the chips. *It does not matter who flipped the chips.*
- Player A gets a point if the chips match.
- Player B gets a point if the chips do not match.

---

1.   From the description of the game, do you and your partner think Flip 2 Chips is a fair game of chance? _____ Explain your reasoning.

# Quiz

Play the game 20 times with your partner. Tally your results below.

| Player A (match) | Player B (no match) |
| --- | --- |
| | |

2. From your results, do you think the game is fair?_____ Explain your reasoning.

Your teacher will set up a master chart on the board. Record your results—the number of matches and the number of nonmatches—on the chart. After all partners have recorded their data, examine the entire class's results.

3. Based on the class's results, do you now think Flip 2 Chips is a fair game?_____ Explain your reasoning.

4. Would you rather rely on your own data or the entire class's data to decide whether the game is fair? _____ Explain your reasoning.

## Check-Up 2

1. The probability of a particular event is $\frac{3}{8}$. What is the probability that the event will not happen? Explain.

2. If two number cubes are tossed over and over again, what sum would you expect to occur most often? Explain.

3. Josh is tossing beanbags randomly onto this game mat. What is the probability of a beanbag landing in an area marked B?

| | | |
|---|---|---|
| **A** | **A** | **B** |
| | **C** | **A** |
| **B** | **B** | |
| **C** | | |

In 4 and 5, use the spinner to the right.

4. What is the probability of the spinner landing in a region marked A?

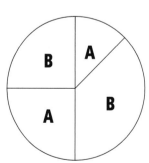

5. What is the probability of the spinner landing in a region marked B?

## Check-Up 2

6. Fifty students in King Middle School were surveyed about their favorite sandwich. Here are the results of the survey:

| Sandwich Preferences | |
| --- | --- |
| Peanut butter | 32 |
| Bologna | 10 |
| Cheese | 7 |
| Tuna fish | 1 |

a. If a student is picked at random from the school, what is the probability that the student's favorite sandwich is peanut butter?

b. If a student is picked at random from the school, what is the probability that the student's favorite sandwich is *not* bologna?

c. If there are 550 students in the school, how many would you expect to say that cheese is their favorite sandwich?

7. A spinner is spun 100 times. The spinner landed on red 61 times and blue 39 times. How might the spinner be divided? Use this circle to draw a spinner that would be likely to give these results.

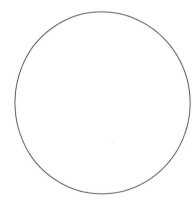

8. Which of the following numbers could not be a probability? Explain your answer.

$\frac{1}{3}$    0    $\frac{8}{9}$    1    $\frac{5}{4}$

Assign these questions as additional homework, or use them as review, quiz, or test questions.

1.  a.  Design a game—other than the Roller Derby game in your book—that uses two number cubes. Explain the rules, and give the number of players and the materials needed.

    b.  Is your game a fair game of chance? Why or why not?

    c.  Make up and answer at least two probability questions about your game.

2.  Each box of Cocoablast cereal includes a Mad Mongo Monster action figure. There are four different action figures, and each figure has an equal chance of being put in a cereal box at the factory. Kalvin is trying to collect at least one of each figure. How many boxes of cereal do you think Kalvin will need to buy before he collects one of each figure? Find a way to investigate this question. Explain your methods and your reasoning.

3.  John is going to flip three coins.

    a.  What is the probability that all three coins will match? Explain your answer.

    b.  What is the probability that there will be at least two heads? Explain your answer.

4.  Think up a bag containing 20 of the same object, such as blocks or marbles, in three or four different colors.

    a.  Describe the contents of the bag you are thinking about.

    b.  Determine the theoretical probability of drawing each color by analyzing the bag's contents.

5.  a.  How many different ways are there to answer a true/false test that has four questions?

    b.  If you were to guess at the four answers for the true/false test, what is the probability of getting all four right?

    c.  If you were to guess at the four answers for the true/false test, what is the probability of getting at least two right?

6.  You have been saving your money for a year and now have enough to buy a new bike. You want to make an informed decision, so you go to the library and read the most recent *Consumer Reports* magazine, which contains an article on models and makes of bikes. (*Consumer Reports* makes recommendations of the best product to buy based on a sampling of hundreds of owners—in this case, bike owners.)

    You also decide to talk to a few of your friends who have bought new bikes in the last year. Four of your friends like a certain model of bike that the *Consumer Reports* article did not highly recommend. Three other friends each recommended the model of bike that they own.

    a.  Would you go with *Consumer Reports* magazine's recommendation, your four friends' recommendation, or an individual friend's recommendation?

    b.  Explain your reasons for deciding whose recommendation you would follow.

# Unit Test

1. Your class has been asked by a game company to test their new, exciting chip game, Flip 3 Chips. You will be playing and analyzing the game. The company wants to know whether the game is fair for all players.

---

**Description of Flip 3 Chips**

*Materials:*  Three chips
- One chip has an X on one side and a Y on the other side.
- One chip has an X on one side and a Z on the other side.
- One chip has a Y on one side and a Z on the other side.

Small cup

*Rules:*  1. Shake the chips in the cup and then pour them out.
2. To score, award points by what shows on the chips. It does not matter who flipped the chips.
- Player A gets a point if any two chips match.
- Player B gets a point if all three chips are different.

---

a. From the description of the game, do you think Flip 3 Chips is a fair game of chance?_____ Explain your answer.

Play the game 20 times. Tally your results below.

| Player A (2 chips match) | Player B (no chips match) |
| --- | --- |
|  |  |

b. From your results, do you think the game is fair?_____ Explain your reasoning.

# Unit Test

**c.** From your results, what is the probability of two chips matching?

**d.** From your results, what is the probability of no chips matching?

Your teacher will set up a master chart on the board. Record your results—the number of two chips matching and the number of no chips matching—on the chart. After all students have recorded their results, examine the entire class's results.

**e.** Based on the class's results, do you now think Flip 3 Chips is a fair game? From your results, do you think the game is fair?_____ Explain your reasoning.

**f.** From the class's results, what is the probability of two chips matching?

**g.** From the class's results, what is the probability of no chips matching?

**h.** What are all the possible outcomes that could result from flipping the chips?

## Unit Test

   **i.**   What is the theoretical probability of two chips matching?

   **j.**   What is the theoretical probability of no chips matching?

   **k.**   How do these two probabilities compare with the class's experimental probabilities?

**2.**  A bag contains one green marble, two yellow marbles, four blue marbles, and five red marbles.

   **a.**   What is the probability of randomly drawing a blue marble from the bag?

   **b.**   What is the probability of not drawing a blue marble?

   **c.**   If you double the number of green, yellow, blue, and red marbles in the bag, what will be the probability of drawing a blue marble?

## Unit Test

**d.** How does your answer for part c compare with your answer for part a? Explain.

**e.** If you add two of each color to the original bag of marbles, what is the probability of drawing a blue marble?

**f.** How does your answer for part e compare with your answer for part a? Explain.

**g.** How many blue marbles would you need to add to the original bag of marbles to make the probability of drawing a blue marble $\frac{1}{2}$?

**3.** A gum machine contains orange, yellow, and purple gum balls. The probability of getting an orange gum ball is $\frac{3}{4}$. The probability of getting a yellow gum ball is $\frac{1}{6}$.

**a.** What is the probability of getting a purple gum ball? Explain how you determined your answer.

**b.** What is the fewest number of gum balls that could be in the machine?

**c.** If there are 36 gum balls in the machine, how many are purple? How many are yellow? How many are orange?

# Notebook Checklist

## Journal Organization

_____ Problems and Mathematical Reflections are labeled and dated.

_____ Work is neat and easy to find and follow.

## Vocabulary

_____ All words are listed.

_____ All words are defined or described.

## Quiz and Check-Ups

_____ Check-Up 1      _____ Quiz

_____ Check-Up 2

## Homework Assignments

_____ _____

_____ _____

_____ _____

_____ _____

_____ _____

_____ _____

_____ _____

_____ _____

_____ _____

_____ _____

_____ _____

_____ _____

_____ _____

_____ _____

# Self-Assessment

**Vocabulary**

Of the vocabulary words I defined or described in my journal, the word _____ best demonstrates my ability to give a clear definition or description.

Of the vocabulary words I defined or described in my journal, the word _____ best demonstrates my ability to use an example to help explain or describe an idea.

**Mathematical Ideas**

1. **a.** In *How Likely Is It?* I learned these things about how to determine the probability that an event will happen:

   **b.** I learned these things about the difference between a possible event and a probable event:

   **c.** Here are page numbers of journal entries that give evidence of what I have learned, along with descriptions of what each entry shows:

2. **a.** These are the mathematical ideas I am still struggling with:

   **b.** This is why I think these ideas are difficult for me:

   **c.** Here are page numbers of journal entries that give evidence of what I am struggling with, along with descriptions of what each entry shows:

**Class Participation**

I contributed to the classroom discussion and understanding of *How Likely Is It?* when I . . .
(Give examples.)

## Answer Keys

### Answers to Check-Up 1

**1.**

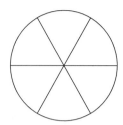

Each section is 60° or $\frac{1}{6}$ of the circle.

**2.** Possible answer:

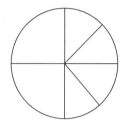

The two large sections are $\frac{1}{4}$ of the circle. The four small sections are $\frac{1}{8}$ of the circle.

**3.** **a.** Possible answers: The sun will rise and set tomorrow. It will snow in Michigan sometime this winter.

**b.** Possible answers: Everyone in our math class will be absent from school tomorrow. The earth will stop rotating.

**c.** 0 or 0%

**4.** **a.** yes; Each time Rachel tosses the coin, it has a 50% possibility of landing heads up.

**b.** no; It is not very likely that a coin will land the same way ten times in a row. There are many ways that a coin can land in ten tosses; ten heads is only one possibility.

---

### For the Teacher: Ten Heads in a Row

The probability of getting ten heads in a row with a fair coin is the probability of getting one head ($\frac{1}{2}$) raised to the power of 10: $(0.5)^{10} = \frac{1}{1024}$.

---

**c.** Statement iii is true, because the coin is a fair coin.

**5.** Statement c is true. When flipping two coins, there are four possible outcomes: HH, HT, TH, and TT. Thus, the probability of getting a match is $\frac{2}{4}$ or 50%, and the probability of not getting a match is $\frac{2}{4}$ or 50%.

# Answer Keys

## Answers to Quiz

1. Answers will vary. This question is not assessing students' ability to analyze the situation but rather to make a conjecture and explain why they think their conjecture makes sense. Credit should be given for the reasoning they use, not for whether they correctly decide that the game is fair.

2. Answers will vary. The results should be close to even but will likely not be exactly ten matches and ten nonmatches. Most pairs will probably obtain results that suggest the game is fair. However, each pair's answer should be evaluated based on their results; if their data are skewed, they may report that the game is unfair. They should be given credit if their results support their explanation.

3. The class's results will most likely suggest the game is fair. Students should not argue that the game is unfair because the number of matches and the number of nonmatches are not exactly even; this type of rationale shows a misconception of experimental probability.

4. The class's data are a better indicator of the experimental probability than the individual data because it incorporates a greater number of trials. The more trials, the better predictor the data is of what is likely to happen. Some pairs may have flipped exactly ten matches and ten nonmatches and therefore believe their results are better. If they argue this point, they still need to address the fact that in most cases the class's data set would be better.

## Answers to Check-Up 2

1. $\frac{5}{8}$

2. 7; There are 36 possible combinations of a roll of two number cubes. Six of the 36 combinations give a sum of 7; $P(\text{sum of } 7) = \frac{6}{36} = \frac{1}{6}$. The next closest are the sums of 6 and 8, with five combinations each; $P(\text{sum of } 6) = P(\text{sum of } 8) = \frac{5}{36}$.

3. $\frac{7}{16}$

4. $\frac{3}{8}$

5. $\frac{5}{8}$

6. a. $\frac{32}{50} = \frac{16}{25}$

   b. $\frac{32}{50} + \frac{7}{50} + \frac{1}{50} = \frac{40}{50} = \frac{4}{5}$

   c. 77, because $\frac{7}{50} = \frac{77}{550}$

7. Possible answer:

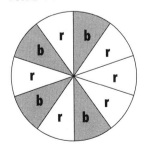

   About $\frac{2}{5}$ should be blue and $\frac{3}{5}$ should be red.

8. $\frac{5}{4}$; All probabilities are numbers from 0 to 1. Since $\frac{5}{4}$ is greater than 1, it can't be a probability.

### Answers to Question Bank

1. Answers will vary.

---

**For the Teacher: Extending Question Bank Question 1**

You could assign this question as a miniproject. Students could exchange and evaluate each other's games.

---

2. Answers will vary. This unit has not addressed the mathematics students need to analyze this problem theoretically, but they should be able to simulate it. For example, students could use four different-colored but otherwise identical items, draw them from a container one at a time (replacing after each draw), and count how many times they must do this until they have drawn all four colors. Or, students could divide a spinner into four equal sections, label each section for the four action figures, and count the spins it takes to get one of each figure.

   Students would need to repeat their experiment until they had enough data to make a reasonable prediction. From their experiences in this unit, they should communicate their understanding that a large number of trials will result in an experimental probability that is a good predictor. Ten trials are too few to count on the results being dependable, and more than 50 is probably too many to expect students to do. The data for ten trials might look like this: 6, 10, 4, 14, 9, 12, 8, 5, 13, 6, which gives an average of 8.7 (or 9) boxes of cereal needed to collect all four figures.

3. **a.** $\frac{2}{8} = \frac{1}{4}$; There are eight possible outcomes, all equally likely: HHH, HHT, HTH, HTT, THH, THT, TTH, and TTT. Only two outcomes (TTT and HHH) have all three coins matching.

   **b.** $\frac{4}{8} = \frac{1}{2}$; Four of the eight outcomes (HHH, HHT, HTH, and THH) include at least two heads.

4. Answers will vary.

5. **a.** There are 16 different ways to answer the questions.

| question 1 | question 2 | question 3 | question 4 |
|------------|------------|------------|------------|
| T | T | T | T |
| T | T | T | F |
| T | T | F | T |
| T | T | F | F |
| T | F | T | T |
| T | F | T | F |
| T | F | F | T |
| T | F | F | F |
| F | T | T | T |
| F | T | T | F |
| F | T | F | T |
| F | T | F | F |
| F | F | T | T |
| F | F | T | F |
| F | F | F | T |
| F | F | F | F |

**b.** P(4 right) $= \frac{1}{16}$

**c.** P(at least 2 right) $= \frac{11}{16}$

6. The recommendations in *Consumer Reports* are based on a very large sample; the friends' recommendations are based on a very small sample. If students argue to follow their friends' recommendations, they are being persuaded by factors such as the desire to be like one's friends and are missing the idea that predictions are best made by considering a large number of trials.

## Answers to Unit Test

1. **a.** Answers will vary. Any answer based on good reasoning is acceptable. This question is not assessing students' ability to analyze the situation but rather to make a conjecture and support that conjecture with sound mathematical reasoning. Credit should be given for the reasoning used.

   **b.** Answers will vary. Most students will obtain results that suggest the game is unfair. Evaluate each student's answer based on the results of the 20 trials.

   **c.** Answers will vary.

   **d.** Answers will vary.

   **e.** The class's results will likely indicate that the game is unfair.

   **f.** Answers will vary.

   **g.** Answers will vary.

| Chip 1 | Chip 2 | Chip 3 | Result | Winner |
|--------|--------|--------|----------|----------|
| X | X | Y | match | player A |
| X | X | Z | match | player A |
| X | Z | Y | no match | player B |
| X | Z | Z | match | player A |
| Y | X | Y | match | player A |
| Y | X | Z | no match | player B |
| Y | Z | Y | match | player A |
| Y | Z | Z | match | player A |

   **h.**

   **i.** P(2 chips matching) $= \frac{6}{8} = \frac{3}{4}$

   **j.** P(no chips matching) $= \frac{2}{8} = \frac{1}{4}$

   **k.** Answers will vary. The class's results will probably be close to the theoretical probabilities.

2. **a.** P(blue) $= \frac{4}{12} = \frac{1}{3}$

   **b.** P(not blue) $= \frac{8}{12} = \frac{2}{3}$

   **c.** P(blue) $= \frac{8}{24} = \frac{1}{3}$

   **d.** The answers are equivalent because the proportion of balls of each color remains the same.

    **e.** P(blue) $= \frac{6}{20} = \frac{3}{10}$

    **f.** The answers are not equivalent. The probability of drawing a blue marble is greater in part a because the proportion of blue balls is greater.

    **g.**    4; then P(blue) $= \frac{8}{16} = \frac{1}{2}$

**3.**   **a.** P(purple) $= \frac{1}{12}$

    **b.** 12

    **c.** purple = 3 gum balls; yellow = 6 gum balls; orange = 27 gum balls

The assessment for *How Likely Is It?* includes a partner quiz. The blackline masters for the quiz appear on pages 69 and 70. Below is a general scoring rubric and specific guidelines of how the rubric can be applied to each of the quiz questions. This is followed by samples of student work and a teacher's comments about how the work was assessed.

## Suggested Scoring Rubric

This rubric awards a maximum of 3 points for each question based on the general guidelines given. Below the general guidelines are specific guidelines for assessing each question.

### General Guidelines

*3 Complete Response*
- Complete, with clear, coherent explanations
- Shows understanding of the mathematical concepts and procedures
- Satisfies all essential conditions of the problem

*2 Reasonably Complete Response*
- Reasonably complete; may lack detail in explanations
- Shows understanding of most of the mathematical concepts and procedures
- Satisfies most of the essential conditions of the problem

*1 Partial Response*
- Incomplete; explanation is insufficient or not understandable
- Shows little understanding of the mathematical concepts and procedures
- Fails to address essential conditions of problem

*0 No Attempt*
- Irrelevant response
- Does not attempt a solution
- Does not address conditions of the problem

### Specific Guidelines for Each Question

*Question 1* Credit should be given for the reasoning used, not for knowing whether the game is fair.

*Question 2* Full credit should be given for explanations that are supported by the data. Although the game is fair, pairs with skewed data may report that the game appears to be unfair. Pairs who believe the game is fair, but who have skewed data, may explain that there are too few trails to make a reasonable decision about the fairness of the game. In both these cases, the explanations should be given full credit.

*Question 3* Full credit should be given for explanations that are supported by the data. The class results will most likely suggest that the game is fair. Students who argue that the game is not fair because the results were not exactly half matching and half not matching, should not be given full credit. This type of rationale shows a misconception about experimental probability.

*Question 4* Students should argue that the class data is a better indicator of probability than data from individual pairs because it considers many more trials. Pairs that flipped exactly 10 matching chips and 10 nonmatching chips might argue that their results are better. Full credit should not be given for such an answer. It is fine for groups to mention that their results were "perfect," but they must also address the fact that, in most cases, the class data would be a better indicator because of the number of trials.

## Sample 1

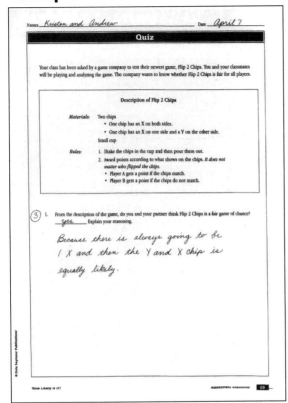

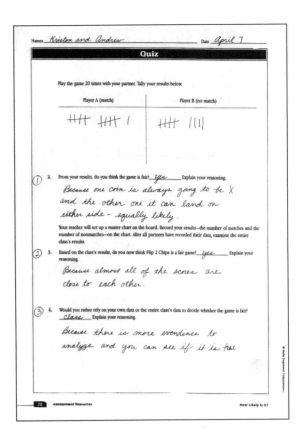

## Sample 2

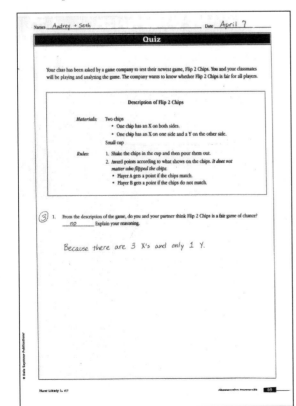

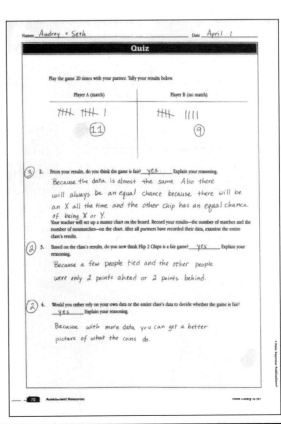

### A Teacher's Comments on Kristen and Andrew's Paper

Kristen and Andrew received all 3 points for both question 1 and question 4. Their answers for these questions are reasonable and clearly stated and show understanding of probability and equally likely events. They received only 1 point for question 2 because they did not discuss what their data suggests about the fairness of the game; they merely repeated their explanation from question 1. They received 2 points for question 3 because, although they considered the results of other pairs, they did not consider what the accumulated data implies about the fairness of the game.

The quiz indicates that Kristen and Andrew have made some sense of probability. They seem to be struggling with what experimental data indicates about the chance of something happening. If I find that others are having trouble using data and interpreting experimental probabilities, I will address this in future lessons. I also want to talk or write to Kristen and Andrew about the importance of reading questions carefully.

### A Teacher's Comments on Audrey and Seth's Paper

Audrey and Seth were given 3 points for question 1 because their explanation is reasonable for this point in the assessment piece. I interpreted their written explanation to mean that more Xs will come up because there are three Xs on the chips and only one Y. I made this interpretation based on the way my students talk about events in class. I know that the communication demonstrated by these two students is weak, but I am trying to focus on what they tell me about the mathematics, keeping in mind that they are still learning about how to communicate their mathematical ideas in writing.

Audrey and Seth were also given 3 points for question 2 because they gave a complete response, showed understanding of the mathematics, and satisfied the conditions of the problem. They received 2 points for question 3 because their answer lacked clarity and, like Kristen and Andrew's answer, failed to address what the accumulated results imply. They received 2 points for question 4 due to lack of clarity.

Audrey and Seth have made some sense of experimental probability. This is evident in how they changed their minds about the fairness of the game based on their results and the results of the class. I want to talk or write to them about communicating their ideas. I will suggest that they read what they have written aloud to see whether it makes sense and clearly communicates what they are thinking. I will also discuss the importance of reading questions carefully and giving complete answers.

# Blackline
# Masters

# Flipping Coins

| June | | | | | |
|---|---|---|---|---|---|
| 1 | 2 | 3 | 4 | 5 | 6 |
| 7 | 8 | 9 | 10 | 11 | 12 | 13 |
| 14 | 15 | 16 | 17 | 18 | 19 | 20 |
| 21 | 22 | 23 | 24 | 25 | 26 | 27 |
| 28 | 29 | 30 | | | | |

| Number of heads | | | | | | | | | | |
|---|---|---|---|---|---|---|---|---|---|---|
| Number of days | 1 | 2 | 3 | 4 | 5 | 6 | 7 | 8 | 9 | 10 |
| Percent heads | | | | | | | | | | |

| Number of heads | | | | | | | | | | |
|---|---|---|---|---|---|---|---|---|---|---|
| Number of days | 11 | 12 | 13 | 14 | 15 | 16 | 17 | 18 | 19 | 20 |
| Percent heads | | | | | | | | | | |

| Number of heads | | | | | | | | | | |
|---|---|---|---|---|---|---|---|---|---|---|
| Number of days | 21 | 22 | 23 | 24 | 25 | 26 | 27 | 28 | 29 | 30 |
| Percent heads | | | | | | | | | | |

# Flipping Coins

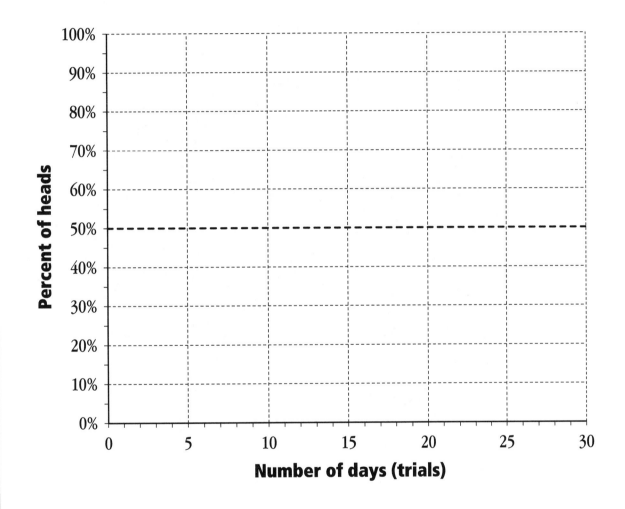

# Kalvin's Spinner

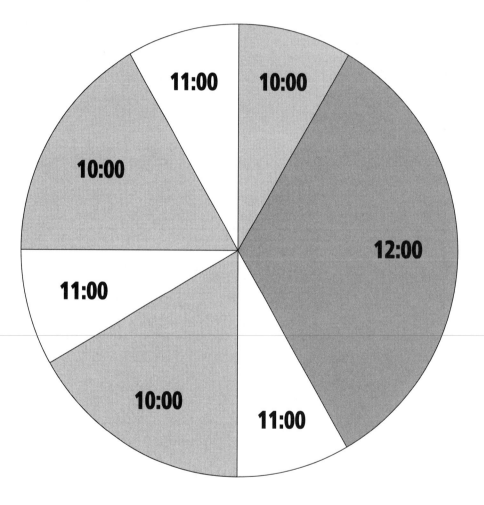

# ACE Question 1

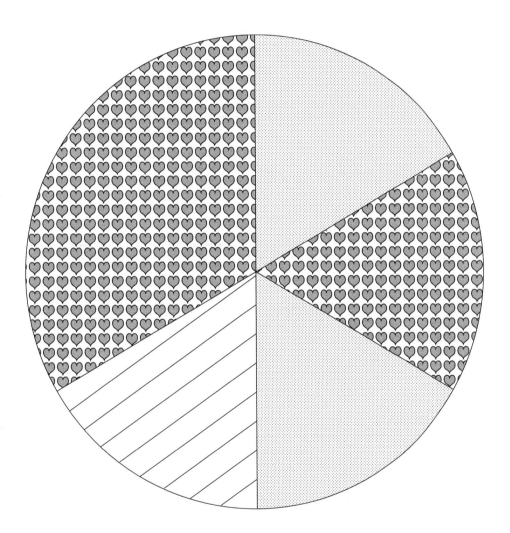

# Roller Derby Game Board

## Roller Derby Game Board

| 1 | 2 | 3 | 4 | 5 | 6 | 7 | 8 | 9 | 10 | 11 | 12 |
|---|---|---|---|---|---|---|---|---|----|----|----|
|   |   |   |   |   |   |   |   |   |    |    |    |

How many days in June do you think Kalvin will eat Cocoa Blast?

Explore this question by flipping a coin 30 times to determine Kalvin's cereal for each morning in June. Use Labsheet 1.1 to help you collect your data.

| June | | | | | | |
|---|---|---|---|---|---|---|
| | **1** | **2** | **3** | **4** | **5** | **6** |
| **7** | **8** | **9** | **10** | **11** | **12** | **13** |
| **14** | **15** | **16** | **17** | **18** | **19** | **20** |
| **21** | **22** | **23** | **24** | **25** | **26** | **27** |
| **28** | **29** | **30** | | | | |

For each day, record the result of the flip (H or T) and the percent of heads so far. Use the data to make a coordinate graph with the days from 1 to 30 on the *x*-axis and the percent of heads so far on the *y*-axis.

In A–H, decide whether the possible resulting events of each action are equally likely, and briefly explain your answer.

| Action | Possible resulting events |
|---|---|
| **A.** You toss a soda can. | The can lands on its side, the can lands upside down, or the can lands right side up. |
| **B.** You roll a number cube. | 1, 2, 3, 4, 5, or 6 |
| **C.** You check the weather in Alaska on a December day. | It snows, it rains, or it does not rain or snow. |
| **D.** The Pittsburgh Steelers play a football game. | The Steelers win, the Steelers lose, or the Steelers tie. |
| **E.** A baby is born. | The baby is a boy or the baby is a girl. |
| **F.** A baby is born. | The baby is right-handed or the baby is left-handed. |
| **G.** You guess on a true/false question. | The answer is right or the answer is wrong. |
| **H.** You shoot a free throw. | You make the basket or you miss. |

Experiment with large and small marshmallows to help you answer these questions:

**A.** Which size marshmallow should Kalvin use to determine which cereal he will eat? Explain your answer.

**B.** Which of the marshmallow's landing positions—end or side— should Kalvin use to represent Cocoablast? Explain your answer.

To conduct your experiment, toss each size of marshmallow 50 times. Keep track of your data carefully. Here is an example of how you might want to organize your data:

|  | Lands on an end | Lands on side |
|---|---|---|
| Large marshmallow | 卌 I | IIII |
| Small marshmallow |  |  |

Use the results of your experiment to help you answer questions A and B.

Conduct an experiment to help you answer these questions:

**A.** Is it possible for Jon to win the game? Is it possible for Tat Ming to win the game? Explain your reasoning.

**B.** Who is more likely to win? Why?

**C.** Is this a fair game of chance? Explain.

To conduct your experiment, toss three coins 30 times. Keep track of the number of times three coins match and the number of times only two coins match. Be sure to organize your data and give reasons for your conclusions.

Conduct an experiment to help you answer these questions.

**A.** Kalvin prefers to go to bed at midnight, so he wants his spinner to land on 12:00 more often than anywhere else. Is it likely that this spinner will allow him to achieve this goal? Explain.

**B.** Suppose Kalvin's father lets him use this spinner to determine his bedtime. What are Kalvin's chances of going to bed at 12:00? Explain how you determined your answer.

To conduct your experiment, use Labsheet 3.1 and a bobby pin or paper clip to make a spinner like Kalvin's. Spin the spinner, and keep track of the data you collect. Continue spinning the spinner and recording data until you are confident about your answers to the questions above.

Play the block-guessing game with your class. Your teacher will act as the host of the game show, and you and your classmates will be the contestants. Keep a record of the number of times each color is drawn. Play the game until you think you can predict with certainty the chances of each color being drawn.

**A.** In your class experiment, how many blue blocks were drawn? Red blocks? Yellow blocks? What was the total number of blocks drawn?

**B.** The probability of drawing a red block can be written as P(red). Find all three probabilities based on the data you collected in your experiment.

P(red) =

P(yellow) =

P(blue) =

Now, your teacher will dump out the blocks so you can see them.

**C.** How many of the blocks are red? Yellow? Blue? How many blocks are there altogether?

**D.** Find the fraction of the total blocks that are red, the fraction that are yellow, and the fraction that are blue.

Your teacher put three yellow blocks, four red blocks, and one blue block in a bucket.

**A.** When you draw a block from the bucket, are the chances equally likely that it will be yellow, red, or blue? Explain your answer.

**B.** What is the total number of blocks? How many blocks of each color are there?

**C.** What is the *theoretical probability* of drawing a blue block? A yellow block? A red block? Explain how you found each answer.

Now, as a class or in groups, take turns drawing a block from the bucket. After each draw, return the block to the bucket. Keep a record of the blocks that are drawn. If you work in a group, take turns drawing blocks until you have 40 trials.

**D.** Based on your data, what is the *experimental probability* of drawing a blue block? A yellow block? A red block?

**E.** Compare the theoretical probabilities you found in part C to the experimental probabilities you found in part D. Are the prob-abilities for each color close? Are they the same? If not, why not?

What are a contestant's chances of winning?

Conduct an experiment to help you answer this question. Keep track of the pairs of colors that are drawn, and make sure you collect enough data to give you good estimates of the probability of drawing each pair. Remember, contestants must guess the color of the block they will pick from each bag. That means you will have to count (a blue from bag 1, a red from bag 2) as a different pair from (a red from bag 1, a blue from bag 2).

**A.** Based on your experiment, what are a contestant's chances of winning?

**B.** List all the possible pairs that can be drawn from the bags. Are each of these pairs equally likely? Explain your answer.

**C.** What is the theoretical probability of each pair being drawn? Explain your answer.

**D.** How do the theoretical probabilities compare with your experimental probabilities? Explain any differences.

What is a good strategy for placing your markers in the 12 columns on the game board?

Play the game at least twice before answering this question. As you play, keep a record of the strategies you use.

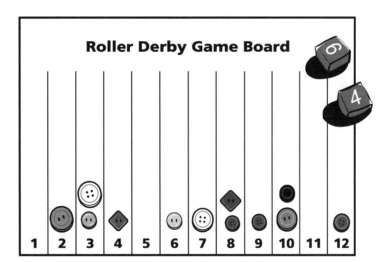

If you play this game once, what is your probability of winning?
To answer this question, do the following two things:

**A.** Create a way to simulate Tawanda's contest, and find the
experimental probability of winning.

**B.** Analyze the different ways you can scratch off two spots, and
find the theoretical probability of winning a prize with one
game card.

What fraction of students in your class can curl their tongues?

With your class, conduct a survey of the students in the class to investigate tongue curling and to answer this question.

Kalvin's mother is pregnant with her third child. Kalvin figured out from studying his family for several generations that his mother and father both have the tongue-curling alleles Tt. Based on what you know about his parent's alleles, what is the probability that Kalvin's new sibling will be able to curl his or her tongue?

Dear Family,

The next unit in your child's course of study in mathematics class this year is *How Likely Is It?* This unit helps students develop an understanding of situations involving probability.

Students will learn to find probabilities in two ways: by conducting trials and collecting experimental data and by analyzing situations to determine theoretical probabilities. As they work, students will be using fractions, decimals, and percents to describe how likely certain events are.

To explore probability, students experiment with coins, number cubes, spinners, and even marshmallows. They will examine simple games of chance to determine whether they are fair. The last investigation in the unit connects to science. Students will examine how probability is used to determine genetic traits such as eye color and tongue-curling ability.

You can help your child see how probability is important in everyday life in several ways:

- With your child, discuss examples of statements or situations in everyday experiences that relate to the likelihood of certain events. Examples are weather forecasting, the chances of a baby being a girl, the chances of your favorite college team winning an NCAA championship, or the likelihood of winning the lottery.

- Look at sports statistics with your child, and ask questions such as how a batting average or a free-throw average can be used to predict the likelihood that the player will get a hit the next time out at bat or make a basket the next time at the free-throw line.

- Look over your child's homework and make sure all questions are answered and that explanations are clear.

If you have any questions or concerns about probability or your child's progress in the class, please feel free to call. All of us here are interested in your child and want to be sure that this year's mathematics experiences are enjoyable and promote a firm understanding of mathematics.

Sincerely,

Estimada familia,

La próxima unidad del programa de matemáticas de su hijo o hija para este curso se llama *How Likely Is It?* (*¿Qué probabilidad hay?*). La misma ayudará a los alumnos a entender situaciones relacionadas con la probabilidad.

Los alumnos aprenderán a hallar probabilidades de dos maneras: una mediante la realización de pruebas y la recogida de datos experimentales y otra mediante el análisis de situaciones para determinar las probabilidades teóricas. Para describir las probabilidades de ciertos sucesos, utilizarán fracciones, decimales y porcentajes.

Para explorar la probabilidad, los alumnos experimentarán con monedas, cubos numerados, ruletas e incluso bombones de merengue. Examinarán sencillos juegos de azar para determinar si son justos. La última investigación de la unidad está relacionada con las ciencias. En ella investigarán cómo usar la probabilidad para determinar ciertos rasgos genéticos como, por ejemplo, el color de los ojos o la capacidad de la lengua para doblarse.

Para ayudar a su hijo o hija a comprender la importancia de la probabilidad en la vida diaria, ustedes pueden hacer lo siguiente:

- Hablen con él o ella sobre algunas afirmaciones o situaciones de la vida cotidiana que estén relacionadas con la probabilidad de ciertos sucesos. Ejemplos de ello son los pronósticos del tiempo, las posibilidades de que nazca una niña, las probabilidades de que su equipo universitario favorito gane el campeonato de la NCAA o bien las posibilidades de ganar la lotería.

- Miren con él o ella las estadísticas deportivas y háganle preguntas como la siguiente: ¿de qué manera puede usarse el promedio de bateo o el promedio de tiros libres para predecir la probabilidad de que el jugador de béisbol consiga un batazo la próxima vez que entre a batear o el jugador de básquetbol consiga encestar la próxima vez que esté en la línea de tiros libres?

- Repasen su tarea para asegurarse de que conteste todas las preguntas y escriba con claridad las explicaciones.

Si ustedes necesitan más detalles o aclaraciones respecto a la probabilidad o sobre los progresos de su hijo o hija en esta clase, no duden en llamarnos. A todos nos interesa su hijo o hija y queremos asegurarnos de que las experiencias matemáticas que tenga este año sean lo más amenas posibles y ayuden a fomentar en él o ella una sólida comprensión de las matemáticas.

Atentamente,

# Additional Practice

### Investigation 1

1. Students at Euler Middle School are talking about ways to raise money for a school party. One student suggests a game called Heads or Tails. In this game, a player pays 50 cents and chooses heads or tails. The player then tosses a fair coin. If the coin matches the player's call, the player wins a prize.

   a. Suppose 100 players play the game. How many of these players would you expect to win?

   b. Suppose the prizes awarded to winners of the Heads or Tails game cost 40 cents each. Based on your answer to part a, how much money would you expect the students to raise if 100 players play the game? Explain your reasoning.

   c. Do you think the Heads or Tails game is an effective game for raising money for the school party? Explain your reasoning.

2. Suppose you toss a fair coin 75 times.

   a. How many times would you expect to get heads?

   b. How many times would you expect to get tails?

   c. Juan tossed a coin 75 times. The coin landed heads up 50 times and tails up 25 times. Can you conclude that the coin is not a fair coin? Explain.

3. Joyce tossed a coin 10 times and recorded an "H" for each head and a "T" for each tail.
   Her results were: H, H, H, H, H, T, T, T, T, T.

   a. If you tossed a fair coin 10 times would you expect to get the same number of heads and tails in the same order that Joyce got? Explain your answer.

   b. Based on the results of Joyce's flips, do you think her coin is fair or not fair? Explain your reasoning.

4. Betty empties her piggy bank, which contains 210 coins, out onto her desk.

   a. How many of the coins would you expect to be heads up?

   b. How many of the coins would you expect to be tails up?

### Investigation 2

1. An ordinary six-sided number cube has the numbers from 1 through 6 on its faces.

   a. If you roll a six-sided number cube, what are the possible outcomes?

   b. Suppose you roll a six-sided number cube 18 times. How many times would you expect to roll a 5? What are you assuming about the possible outcomes?

   c. Takashi and Glen are playing a game. For each turn, a number cube is rolled. If the roll is an even number, Takashi gets a point. If the roll is odd, Glen gets a point. Is this a fair game? Explain your reasoning.

2. Patrick counted the cars that drove by his house over a 5-minute period. He counted a total of 27 cars.

   a. If Patrick had counted cars for an hour, about how many would you expect him to have counted?

   b. Suppose that at the same time of the day exactly one week later, Patrick counts cars over a 20-minute period. About how many cars would you expect him to count?

   c. If Patrick started counting cars after school at about 3 P.M., would you expect him to count more, fewer, or about the same number of cars than if he started counting at 5 P.M.? Explain your reasoning.

### Investigation 3

1.  Use your angle ruler and the spinner at the right to answer the following questions.

    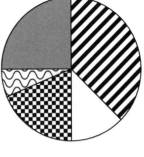

    a.  What fraction of the area of the spinner is gray?

    b.  What fraction is checked?

    c.  What fraction is marked with diagonal lines?

    d.  What fraction is marked with wavy lines?

    e.  What fraction is unmarked?

    f.  If you were to spin the spinner 40 times, how many times would you expect it to land on the diagonally-marked region? Explain your reasoning.

    g.  If you were to spin the spinner 40 times, how many times would you expect it to land on the gray region?

    h.  If you were to spin the spinner 40 times, how many times would you expect it to land on the unmarked region?

2.  Ralph would like to make a spinner with three different colored regions so that a person would expect to spin the first color half the time, the second color one-third of the time, and the third color one-fourth of the time. Is it possible to make such a spinner? Explain why or why not.

3.  Glenda has designed a spinner with blue, red, and green sections. The chances of spinning blue on Glenda's spinner are 50%, the chances of spinning red are 20%, and the chances of spinning green are 30%. Suppose you spin Glenda's spinner 50 times.

    a.  How many times would you expect to spin blue?

    b.  How many times would you expect to spin red?

    c.  How many times would you expect to spin green?

4.  Use the spinner at right to answer the following questions.

    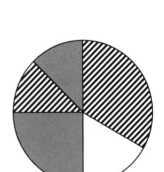

    a.  What fraction of the area of the spinner is shaded gray?

    b.  What fraction is unshaded?

    c.  What fraction is marked with diagonal lines?

    d.  Suppose you spun the spinner 72 times.

        i.  How many times would you expect to spin gray?

        ii.  How many times would you expect to spin the unshaded region?

        iii.  How many times would you expect to spin diagonals?

**Investigation 4**

1. A bag contains 20 pieces of candy. There are 8 grape pieces, 7 cherry pieces, and 5 lemon pieces.

   **a.** One piece is drawn from the bag. Find the theoretical probability of drawing each flavor.

   **i.** P(grape) =             **ii.** P(cherry) =             **iii.** P(lemon) =

   **b.** Write each of the probabilities from part a as a percent.

   **i.** P(grape) =             **ii.** P(cherry) =             **iii.** P(lemon) =

   **c.** Suppose 2 grape pieces, 1 cherry piece and 1 lemon piece are removed from the bag. What is the theoretical probability of drawing each flavor now?

   **i.** P(grape) =             **ii.** P(cherry) =             **iii.** P(lemon) =

   **d.** In part c, what is the theoretical probability of not drawing lemon?

2. A can contains eight chips. Three chips are gray, four are checkered, and one is white.

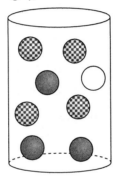

   **a.** What is the probability of drawing a white chip?

   **b.** What is the probability of drawing a checkered chip?

   **c.** What is the probability of drawing a gray chip?

   **d.** What is the probability of not drawing a white chip?

   **e.** What is the probability of not drawing a gray chip?

3. A bucket contains 24 blue, green, red, and yellow blocks. The theoretical probabilities of drawing a blue, green, or red block are: P(blue) = $\frac{1}{12}$, P(green) = $\frac{1}{8}$, P(red) = $\frac{1}{3}$.

   **a.** How many blue blocks are in the bucket?

   **b.** How many green blocks are in the bucket?

   **c.** How many red blocks are in the bucket?

   **d.** How many yellow blocks are in the bucket?

   **e.** What is the probability of drawing a yellow block?

   **f.** What is the probability of not drawing a yellow block?

### Investigation 5

1. The Four-by-Four game involves two four-sided dice. Each die has four triangular faces numbered 1, 2, 3, and 4. The result of a roll is the number on the face touching the table.

    To play the game, players take turns rolling the dice and adding the results. If the sum is odd, the first player gets a point. If the sum is even, the second player gets a point.

    a. Find a systematic way to list all the possible number pairs that can be rolled and the sum for each pair.

    b. Is Four-by-Four a fair game? Explain your reasoning.

    c. Which sum is most likely, and what is its probability?

    d. What is the probability of rolling a sum of 6?

    e. What is the probability of rolling a sum of 3?

    f. What is the probability of *not* rolling a sum of 8? Explain your reasoning.

2. Suppose the rules of Four-by-Four are kept the same except that instead of finding the sum of the two numbers rolled, you find the product.

    a. List all the possible products that can be rolled.

    b. Is this version of Four-by-Four a fair game? Explain your reasoning.

    c. Which product is most likely, and what is its probability?

    d. What is the probability of rolling a product of 5?

    e. What is the probability of rolling a product of 12?

    f. What is the probability of *not* rolling a product of 2?

    g. What is the probability of rolling a product greater than 3?

## Investigation 6

1. A game is played by rolling a four-sided die and a six-sided die and finding the sum of the numbers rolled. A player wins by rolling a sum of 2, 3, 4, 9, or 10; otherwise, the player loses.

   a. List all the possible number pairs that can be rolled and find the sum of each pair.

   b. Is this game fair or unfair? Explain your reasoning.

   c. What is the probability of rolling a sum of 7?

   d. What is the probability of rolling a sum of 4?

   e. What is the probability of *not* rolling a sum of 9?

   f. If you played this game 48 times, how many times would you expect to win? How many times would you expect to lose?

   g. Suppose the game costs 25 cents to play, and if you win you get 50 cents. Suppose you play the game 48 times. Use your answers from part f to answer the following questions:

      i. How much money would it cost to play 48 times?

      ii. How much money would you expect to win?

      iii. What would you expect your final win or loss to be after playing the game 48 times?

2. A game called Part or Whole? uses the two spinners shown below.

   **Spinner A**          **Spinner B**

   One player spins spinner A and the other spins spinner B. The number spun on spinner A is then divided by the number spun on spinner B. If the result is a fraction, the player spinning spinner A gets a point. If the quotient is a whole number, the player spinning spinner B gets a point.

   a. List all the possible number pairs that can be spun with two spinners and find the quotient of each pair.

   b. Is Part or Whole? a fair game? Explain your reasoning.

   c. What is the probability of spinning a quotient of 1?

   d. What is the probability of spinning a quotient of 3?

   e. What is the probability of *not* spinning a quotient of $\frac{2}{3}$?

### Investigation 7

1. A new family with two children has just moved in across the street from Mary. Assuming that it is equally likely for a person to be born female or male, answer the following questions.

   a. What are all the possible outcomes (that is, each child being a boy or girl) of having two children? List the outcomes in the form (gender of first child, gender of second child).

   b. What is the probability that both children are girls?

   c. What is the probability that one child is a boy and the other is a girl?

   d. What is the probability that the oldest child is a boy?

2. Assuming that it is equally likely for a child to be born a girl or a boy, answer the following questions.

   a. Suppose a family has three children. List all the possible outcomes for the genders of the children.

   b. If a family has three children, what is the probability that all three children are girls? That all three children are boys?

   c. What is the probability of having two girls and one boy?

   d. What is the probability of having two boys and one girl?

   e. Josh has a younger brother, and his mother is pregnant with a third baby. What is the probability that Josh's mother will have another boy? Explain your reasoning.

## Answer Keys

### Investigation 1

1. a. 50     b. $30     c. Answers will vary.

2. a. 37 or 38     b. 37 or 38     c. Juan's coin appears to be unfair. He has tossed the coin a large number of times and the fraction of heads is not close to $\frac{1}{2}$.

3. a. For a large number of tosses, about half the results will be heads. However, with only ten tosses, the results may be very different from Joyce's. Since many orders are possible, it is likely that the order of the results will be different from Joyce's.

   b. Although Joyce got half heads and half tails, ten tosses is not enough to determine whether the coin is fair.

4. a. About 105     b. About 105

### Investigation 2

1. a. 1, 2, 3, 4, 5, 6     b. About three 5s—assuming that all possible outcomes are equally likely.

   c. Yes, there are the same number of even and odd outcomes.

2. a. 324     b. 108

   c. Probably fewer since traffic generally becomes heavier near the time people tend to finish work (i.e., about 5).

### Investigation 3

1. a. $\frac{1}{4}$     b. $\frac{1}{6}$     c. $\frac{3}{8}$     d. $\frac{1}{12}$

   e. $\frac{1}{8}$     f. 15     g. 10     h. 5

2. No, the chances add up to $\frac{1}{2} + \frac{1}{3} + \frac{1}{4} = \frac{26}{24} > 1$.

3. a. 25     b. 10     c. 15

4. a. $\frac{3}{8}$     b. $\frac{1}{6}$     c. $\frac{11}{24}$

   d. i. 27     ii. 12     iii. 33

### Investigation 4

1. a. i. $\frac{8}{20}$     ii. $\frac{7}{20}$     iii. $\frac{5}{20}$

   b. i. 40%     ii. 35%     iii. 25%

   c. i. $\frac{6}{16}$     ii. $\frac{6}{16}$     iii. $\frac{4}{16}$

   d. $\frac{12}{16}$

**2. a.** $\frac{1}{8}$  **b.** $\frac{4}{8}$  **c.** $\frac{3}{8}$  **d.** $\frac{7}{8}$  **e.** $\frac{5}{8}$

**3. a.** 2  **b.** 3  **c.** 8

  **d.** 11  **e.** $\frac{11}{24}$  **f.** $\frac{13}{24}$

## Investigation 5

**1. a.**

| + | 1 | 2 | 3 | 4 |
|---|---|---|---|---|
| 1 | 2 | 3 | 4 | 5 |
| 2 | 3 | 4 | 5 | 6 |
| 3 | 4 | 5 | 6 | 7 |
| 4 | 5 | 6 | 7 | 8 |

**b.** Fair; There is an equal number of even and odd outcomes.

**c.** 5, $P(5) = \frac{4}{16}$  **d.** $\frac{3}{16}$

**e.** $\frac{2}{16}$  **f.** $\frac{15}{16}$, because $P(8) = \frac{1}{16}$

**2. a.**

| × | 1 | 2 | 3 | 4 |
|---|---|---|---|---|
| 1 | 1 | 2 | 3 | 4 |
| 2 | 2 | 4 | 6 | 8 |
| 3 | 3 | 6 | 9 | 12 |
| 4 | 4 | 8 | 12 | 16 |

**b.** The game is not fair. There are 12 even outcomes and only 4 odd outcomes.

**c.** 4, $P(4) = \frac{3}{16}$  **d.** 0  **e.** $\frac{2}{16}$

**f.** $\frac{14}{16}$  **g.** $\frac{11}{16}$

## Investigation 6

**1. a.**

| + | 1 | 2 | 3 | 4 | 5 | 6 |
|---|---|---|---|---|---|----|
| 1 | 2 | 3 | 4 | 5 | 6 | 7 |
| 2 | 3 | 4 | 5 | 6 | 7 | 8 |
| 3 | 4 | 5 | 6 | 7 | 8 | 9 |
| 4 | 5 | 6 | 7 | 8 | 9 | 10 |

**b.** Unfair; $P(\text{win}) = \frac{8}{24}$, $P(\text{lose}) = \frac{16}{24}$

**c.** $\frac{4}{24}$  **d.** $\frac{3}{24}$

**e.** $\frac{22}{24}$  **f.** win 16, lose 32

**g.** **i.** $12  **ii.** $8  **iii.** Expect to lose $4

**2. a.**

| ÷ | 1 | 2 | 3 | 4 | 5 | 6 | 7 | 8 |
|---|---|---|---|---|---|---|---|---|
| 1 | 1 | 2 | 3 | 4 | 5 | 6 | 7 | 8 |
| 2 | $\frac{1}{2}$ | 1 | $\frac{3}{2}$ | 2 | $\frac{5}{2}$ | 3 | $\frac{7}{2}$ | 4 |
| 3 | $\frac{1}{3}$ | $\frac{2}{3}$ | 1 | $\frac{4}{3}$ | $\frac{5}{3}$ | 2 | $\frac{7}{3}$ | $\frac{8}{3}$ |
| 4 | $\frac{1}{4}$ | $\frac{2}{4}$ | $\frac{3}{4}$ | 1 | $\frac{5}{4}$ | $\frac{6}{4}$ | $\frac{7}{4}$ | 2 |

**b.** Fair; There are the same number of whole and fraction quotients possible.

**c.** $\frac{4}{32}$  **d.** $\frac{2}{32}$

**e.** $\frac{31}{32}$

## Investigation 7

1.  a. (male, male), (male, female), (female, female), (female, male)

    b. $\frac{1}{2}$

    c. $\frac{1}{2}$

    d. $\frac{1}{2}$

2.  a. (male, male, male), (male, male, female), (male, female, male), (male, female, female), (female, male, male), (female, male, female), (female, female, male), (female, female, female)

    b. $\frac{1}{8}$, $\frac{1}{8}$       c. $\frac{3}{8}$       d. $\frac{3}{8}$

    e. The probability would be $\frac{1}{2}$ since each child is equally likely to be a boy or girl (although the probability of having 3 children who are all boys is $\frac{1}{8}$).

**certain event** An event that is bound to happen—for example, the sun rising tomorrow. The probability of a certain outcome is 1.

**chances** The likelihood that something will happen. For example, "What are the chances that it will rain tomorrow?"

**equally likely events** Two or more events that have the same chance of happening. For example, when you toss a fair coin, heads and tails are equally likely; each has a 50% chance of happening. When you toss a tack, it is not equally likely that it will land on its side as on its head. It is more likely to land on its side.

**event** A set of outcomes. For example, when two coins are tossed, getting two matching coins is an event consisting of the outcomes HH and TT.

**experimental probability** A probability that is found by experimenting. Experimental probabilities are used to predict what might happen over the long run. For example, you could find the experimental probability of getting a head when you toss a coin by tossing the coin several times and keeping track of the outcomes. The experimental probability would be the ratio of the number of heads to the total number of trials.

**fair game** A game in which each player has the same chance of winning. A game that is not fair can be made fair by adjusting the scoring system. For example, suppose you play a game in which two coins are tossed. You score one point when both coins land heads up. Otherwise, your opponent scores one point. The probability that you will score is $\frac{1}{4}$, and the probability that your opponent will score is $\frac{3}{4}$. To make the game fair, you should get three points each time you score, and your opponent should get only one point for a score.

**favorable outcome** An outcome in which you are interested. A favorable outcome is sometimes called a *success*. For example, when you toss two coins to find the probability of the coins matching, HH and TT are favorable outcomes.

**impossible event** an event that cannot happen. For example, the probability of putting a quarter in a gumball machine and getting the moon is zero.

**outcome** A possible result of an action. For example, when one number cube is rolled, the possible outcomes are 1, 2, 3, 4, 5, and 6.

**possible** A word used to describe an event that can happen. "Possible" does not imply anything about how likely the outcome is. For example, it is *possible* to toss a coin 200 times and get heads every time, but it is not at all likely.

**probability** A number between 0 and 1 that describes the likelihood that an event will occur. For example, if a bag contains a red marble, a white marble, and a blue marble, then the probability of drawing a red marble is $\frac{1}{3}$.

**probable** Another way to say *likely*. An event that is probable is likely to happen.

**random events** Events that are uncertain when viewed individually but which may exhibit a regular pattern when observed over many trials. For example, when you roll a number cube, you have no way of knowing what the next roll will be, but you know that, over the long run, you will roll each number about the same number of times.

**theoretical probability** A probability found by analyzing a situation mathematically. If all the outcomes are equally likely, you can first list all the possible outcomes, and then find the ratio of the number of outcomes you are interested in to the total number of outcomes. For example, there are 36 possible equally likely outcomes (number pairs) when two number cubes are rolled. Of these outcomes, 6 have a sum of 7, so the probability of rolling a sum of 7 is $\frac{6}{36}$, or $\frac{1}{6}$.

**trial** One round of an experiment.

# Index

# Index

Labsheets, 90–94
Law of Large Numbers, 1c
Line plot, prediction from, 38
Looking Back and Looking Ahead:
 Unit Reflections, 64d–64g

Materials
 complete list, 1f
 for Investigation 1, 4b
 for Investigation 2, 13f
 for Investigation 3, 21d
 for Investigation 4, 28d
 for Investigation 5, 41f
 for Investigation 6, 48f
 for Investigation 7, 56d
Mathematical content, 1b–1c
Mathematical goals, 1d
 A First Look at Chance, 4b
 Analyzing Games of Chance, 41f
 More About Games of Chance, 48f
 More Experiments with Chance, 13f
 Probability and Genetics, 56d
 Theoretical Probabilities, 28d
 Using Spinners to Predict Chance, 21d
Mathematical Highlights, 4
Mathematical Reflections, 13, 21, 28, 41, 48, 56, 64

Original Rebus technique, 41, 56
Outcome, 21c, 31
Overview, 1a

Pacing Chart, 1h
Possible event, 16, 21c
Possible outcome, 4, 21c, 31
Prediction, 4
 ACE, 26–27, 35–40, 44–47, 51–55, 61–63
 from a bar graph, 19
 from a line plot, 38
 using experimental probability, 21d, 22–23, 28a–28c, 28d, 29–34, 41a–41d
 using theoretical probability, 28d, 29–34, 41a–41d, 41f, 42–43, 48a–48c, 48f, 49–50, 56a–56b, 56d, 57–60, 64a–64c

Probability, 1a, 1b–1c, 29
 ACE, 9–12, 17–20, 26–27, 35–40, 44–47, 51–55, 61–63
 bias in, 13a
 certain event, 18
 computing, 28d, 31–34, 41a–41d
 equally likely events, 4, 4b, 7–8, 13c–13d
 experimental, 4b, 5–7, 13a–13d, 14–16, 21d, 22–23, 28a–28c, 28d, 29–34, 41a–41d
 flipping a coin, 4b, 5–8, 13a–13d
 game analysis, 41f, 42–43, 48a–48c
 genetics and, 4, 56d, 57–60, 64a–64c
 impossible event, 18
 from a line plot, 38
 outcome, 21c, 31
 possible outcomes, 4, 21c, 31
 prediction with, 21d, 22–23, 28a–28c, 28d, 29–34, 41a–41b, 41f, 42–43, 48a–48c, 48f, 49–50, 56a–56b, 56d, 57–60, 64a–64c
 relative-frequency interpretation of, 1b
 theoretical, 28d, 29–34, 41a–41d, 41f, 42–43, 48a–48c, 48f, 49–50, 56a–56b, 56d, 57–60, 64a–64c
 tossing a marshmallow, 13f, 14–15, 21a–21b
Probable event, 16, 21b–21c
Problem-solving goals, 1d
 A First Look at Chance, 4b
 Analyzing Games of Chance, 41f
 More About Games of Chance, 48f
 More Experiments with Chance, 13f
 Probability and Genetics, 56d
 Theoretical Probabilities, 28d
 Using Spinners to Predict Chance, 21d

Random, 13a, 28d, 31, 41d
Rebus Scenario technique, 7, 14
Relative frequency, interpretation of probability, 1b
Resources, 1g

Simulation, scratch-off game, 4, 48f, 49–50, 56a–56b
Systematic bias, 13a